Mothers Against Drunk Driving

This special edition of the "Food Writers' Favorites: Salads" benefits MADD. Before enjoying the many recipes that follow, please take a few minutes to read over the prefatory material. It explains the steps you can take to prevent drunk driving, provides a history of MADD, and recaps many of the programs and services available through the organization. After reading these pages, MADD hopes you will take a more active part in making the roads safer for all of us.

"THE MISSION OF MOTHERS AGAINST DRUNK DRIVING IS TO STOP DRUNK DRIVING AND TO SUPPORT VICTIMS OF THIS VIOLENT CRIME."

Two of every five Americans will be involved in an alcohol-related crash in their lifetime. In 1989, an estimated 22,415 people were killed and 345,000 injured as the result of alcohol- and other drug-impaired driving crashes. Through your support and involvement, we can eliminate this senseless crime.

HOW CAN YOU HELP PREVENT DRUNK DRIVING?

Drunk driving is a crime. There are several ways you can help reduce the tragic results of alcohol- and other drug-impaired driving.

- Do not refer to incidents caused by alcohol- and other drug-impaired drivers as "accidents." These crashes are not accidental because they result from two clear choices: (1) to consume alcohol or use other drugs; and (2) to drive.

- Never drink and drive and never allow a friend to drink and drive.

- Speak out against alcohol- and other drug-impaired driving in your community.

- Support legislation to reform drunk driving laws. Contact your local, county, state and federal officials to show your interest and support.

- Monitor drunk driving cases from the initial report by the arresting officer through the judicial process in your community or county. Is the process working? Report what you find to the media, your legislators and state or local MADD officials.

- Designate a driver BEFORE you leave the house if your outing involves drinking. And, encourage your friends to always do the same.

- Start educating your children early with the truth about the dangers of alcohol and other drugs.

- Refuse to serve alcohol to any young person until he or she is 21 years of age. It's the law.

- Respect child endangerment laws, and set a good example. Don't drink and drive, particularly with an under 21 person in the vehicle.
- Remember that alcohol — including beer, wine, wine coolers and liquor — is a drug which when consumed leads to impairment.
- Understand that your ability to think clearly and react appropriately can be impaired by alcohol and other drugs long before you become visibly intoxicated.
- Remember that cold showers, coffee or exercise do not lower the level of intoxication. Only time does that — alcohol burns off much more slowly than it is consumed.
- Report suspected drunk drivers promptly to the police.

The National Highway Traffic Safety Administration offers several ways to identify suspected drunk drivers. Alcohol- and other drug-impaired drivers frequently:

- Follow other vehicles too closely or drive with their headlights off at night;
- Drink in the vehicle or drive with the face close to the windshield;
- Weave or zig-zag across the road or drive into opposing traffic;
- Drive slower than 10 m.p.h. below the speed limit;
- Use turn signals that are inconsistent with driving actions or stop in a traffic lane.

If you see a suspected drunk driver, **DO NOT:**

- Attempt to stop the vehicle, or to follow it if the driver is exceeding the posted speed limit;
- Disregard traffic signals if you are following the vehicle;
- Follow the vehicle too closely — the driver may stop suddenly;
- Attempt to detain the drunk driver if he or she stops.

But, you **SHOULD** *call the nearest law enforcement agency and:*

- Tell them you want to report a drunk driver;
- Give the exact location (identify the street or road and direction in which the vehicle is traveling);
- Give a description of the vehicle (license plate number, color, make, model);
- Describe how the vehicle is being driven.

THE HISTORY OF MADD

MADD was founded in California in 1980. An aggressive grassroots campaign resulted in California passing the toughest drunk driving laws in the country at that time.

This astounding success was only the beginning. MADD soon grew into a nationwide organization with almost 3,000,000 members and supporters.

Today, thousands of concerned citizens are involved in more than 400 chapters in the United States with affiliates in Canada, Australia, New Zealand, and Great Britain. MADD is made up of men and women of all ages who share a common concern for safety on our roads.

Since MADD's founding, more than 1,200 anti-drunk driving laws have been enacted nationwide. The rights of victims and survivors of alcohol- and other drug-related crashes are now viewed more equitably in a criminal justice system that only a few years ago paid little attention to them.

MADD PROGRAMS

Community Programs

MADD develops programs throughout the year to promote public awareness and raise the nation's consciousness about the dangers of alcohol- and other drug-impaired driving.

PROJECT RED RIBBON was created by MADD in 1986 to change the meaning of "tie one on." MADD asks drivers to tie a red ribbon to a visible location on their vehicles between Thanksgiving and New Year's Day to show their commitment to drive safe and sober throughout the year. Please take part in this simple but effective program during the holiday season.

Keep It a Safe Summer (K.I.S.S.) Campaign spreads the word that summer months can be the most dangerous. The *Family Vacation Pack* is filled with safety tips and activities for the entire family. Help MADD keep it a safe (and sober) summer on our nation's roads and waterways.

Designated Driver is a program with a simple point: if you choose to drink, bring along a friend who is not drinking to safely drive you home. You can help promote the program by always using a designated driver and offering to be the designated driver for your friends.

Candlelight Vigils remind us of the thousands of loved ones killed or injured in drunk driving crashes. Please attend the *Candlelight Vigil of Remembrance and Hope* in your community to show your support for a less violent future.

Youth Programs

It is illegal for anyone under the age of 21 to be served or to consume alcohol in every state in the nation. Since the national minimum drinking age was implemented, the proportion of drivers under 21 involved in alcohol-related crashes has dramatically declined from 28% in 1982 to 17% in 1989.

Young people today receive many "mixed messages." MADD's message to this group is clear: drinking under the age of 21 is unacceptable and illegal. MADD has developed programs to educate young people how to avoid dangerous situations involving alcohol and other drugs.

Operation Prom/Graduation is a nationwide program designed to make prom and graduation nights memorable occasions, not memorials. It focuses on promoting chemical-free messages and events for high school students. MADD provides "how to" materials to teens and parents on conducting these activities during this special time and throughout the year. Please support *Operation Prom/Graduation* and other sober celebrations for teens in your community.

MADD Poster/Essay Contest invites students in grades 1-12 to use their creative skills to deliver strong messages against drinking and driving. English and Spanish language entries are welcome and local first place entries compete nationally. Contact MADD's Youth Programs Department for information and this year's theme.

The MADD Student Library is published annually to provide information about the impact of alcohol and other drugs on young people as well as the consequences of impaired driving. It includes statistics, articles on topics such as peer pressure, and a bibliography on resources for highway safety issues. Check your school library to be sure they have a current copy on file.

Friends Keep Friends Alive! is an educational comic book which stresses positive peer support. It also teaches children how to say "no" to drinking and riding with someone who has been drinking. It is available in both English and Spanish versions.

National Youth Conferences — MADD and the National Association of Broadcasters hosted national training and networking events in Washington, D.C. in 1990 for teen and adult leaders from across the nation. These conferences focused national attention on teen impaired driving problems *and* solutions. A third conference is planned for July, 1992.

PUBLIC POLICY AND LEGISLATIVE GOALS

During its 10th Anniversary in 1990, MADD renewed its focus on two primary goals: aiding the victims of alcohol- and other drug-related crashes and reducing the incidence of impaired driving.

20 x 2000

Alcohol-related fatalities account for approximately 50% of all traffic fatalities, in spite of a nearly 20 percent reduction since 1980. MADD's goal is to reduce that number by an additional 20% by the year 2000. MADD urges you, and all levels of government, to support this effort by focusing on objectives in these five areas.

Youth Issues: Reducing the number of young people involved in alcohol- and other drug-impaired driving incidents requires more than enacting a minimum drinking age of 21. Alcohol-free areas should be maintained for schools and youth functions, young people must be educated about hazards of alcohol and other drugs, and adults who supply alcohol and other drugs to anyone under the age of 21 must be penalized appropriately, as well as youths who commit such offenses.

Enforcement: Effective tools are available to enforce DWI laws. We must support the use of sobriety checkpoints, preliminary breath tests and passive alcohol sensors, a *per se* limit at an appropriate level such as .08, mandatory Blood Alcohol Content (BAC) testing when crashes result in injury or loss of life, and limits on open alcohol containers in vehicles.

Sanctions: Appropriate sanctions are effective deterrents to DWI crime. Sanctions against alcohol- and other drug-impaired driving that have proven effective include administrative license revocation and mandatory jail time for repeat offenders. Other approaches that may reduce repeat offenses include license plate/vehicle confiscation, increasingly severe penalties for subsequent convictions, and elimination of charge reduction negotiations. Minimum-security facilities to incarcerate DWI offenders should be developed and should provide education and treatment. DWI offenses involving death or serious injury, or when the driver leaves the scene of such a crash, should be felonies and receive appropriately severe penalties. Improvement in monitoring DWI offenses from the time of arrest through the disposition of the case in court is necessary to identify and better deal with multiple offenders. This would also provide better documentation of the DWI problem and effective solutions that are being implemented on a state and national basis.

Self-Sufficient Programs: MADD advocates channeling DWI fines, fees and other assessments, including user fees such as alcohol excise taxes, to ensure consistent, long term funding for comprehensive anti-drunk driving law enforcement.

Responsible Marketing and Service of Alcohol: Increased responsibility in the marketing and serving of alcoholic beverages is imperative. MADD does not call for legislated limits on beverage advertising but strongly urges the alcohol industry to monitor its own efforts to avoid any depictions of dangerous or illegal use of alcohol, including appeals to anyone under the age of 21. Any beverage promotions that encourage excessive consumption, such as "happy hours," should be ended. Programs that encourage responsibility, such as the *Designated Driver*, should be encouraged. Alcohol advertising should also bear appropriate warnings about potential driving impairment and Age 21 limits.

Victim Issues

MADD is the largest anti-drunk driving victim assistance organization in the world. Because victims are frequently overburdened — financially and emotionally — as the result of alcohol- and other drug-impaired crashes, MADD has adopted the following public policy objectives.

Amendments for Victim Rights: Statutory Bills of Rights are only sporadically enforced but State Constitutional Amendments for Victim Rights would offer victims the constitutional right to be informed of, present at, and heard during the criminal justice process.

Bankruptcy Protection for Victims: Persons who kill or injure others as a result of alcohol- or other drug-impaired driving would not have the right to file bankruptcy in order to avoid paying restitution or civil judgments to their victims.

Compensation for Victims: Alcohol- and other drug-impaired crash victims would not be excluded from any State Crime Victim Compensation Program and would have the same eligibility requirements as victims of other violent crimes.

Dram Shop Recovery: Victims would have the right to seek financial recovery from establishments that irresponsibly provide alcohol to anyone under the age of 21 or serve alcohol to anyone past the point of intoxication.

Endangerment of Children Sanctions: Enhanced sanctions against convicted drunk drivers would be enforced when the offender was driving with a child in the vehicle.

MADD VICTIM SERVICES

Each of the 22,415 fatalities and 345,000 injuries incurred yearly is a unique and irreplaceable individual with a name, a family, and dreams that must now go unfulfilled. Each represents far more than a faceless number to his or her family and friends, who are now caught in the tragic ripple effect set off by each crash.

Crisis Intervention: Alcohol- and other drug-related crashes create a critical period in the lives of victims. MADD victim advocates provide emotional support to help victims cope with their grief and anger. In addition, victims receive printed materials to help them understand the grieving process and guide them through the criminal justice system.

Victim Support: MADD brings victims together in victim support groups to discuss their feelings and futures. Victims offer each other unique understanding and reassurance.

Victim Advocacy: Victims are offered a thorough explanation of the judicial process. MADD advocates clarify victim rights, accompany victims to court when necessary and follow-up on the sentencing of offenders. MADD offers 40-hour Beginning and Advanced Institutes to train victim advocates. MADD offers the *Victim Information Pamphlet* to inform victims about their rights in court proceedings and *Financial Recovery After A Drunk Driving Crash* to inform them about victim compensation, insurance and civil suits. The _MADDVOCATE_ magazine provides up-to-date information for victims and victim advocates.

Victim Impact Panels: Judges or probation officers order convicted drunk drivers to attend a Victim Impact Panel as a component of their sentencing. The panel is composed of three or four victims of drunk driving crashes who tell their stories simply and from the heart. The goal of the program is to enable the offenders to understand their crime from the victim's perspective and choose never again to drink and drive.

Information and Referral: MADD chapters refer victims to other agencies that offer financial and legal information, as well as professional counseling, as requested.

1-800 VICTIM CRISIS LINE: To facilitate victim support, a toll-free hot line provides information in times of crises involving drunk driving.

MADD AND YOU

Grassroots activism is the force behind MADD. Your unyielding determination, commitment, energy, courage and creativity, reduces the number of deaths and injuries from alcohol- and other drug-related driving.

You are helping us create a less violent future. Together we are making a difference because *WE ARE IN IT FOR LIVES.*

- Be responsible for your own thinking and actions about drunk driving — *DON'T DRINK AND DRIVE.*

- Encourage your family and friends to be responsible for their thinking and actions about drunk driving — *FRIENDS DON'T LET FRIENDS DRIVE DRUNK.*

- Be informed about the issue of drunk driving. Make yourself knowledgeable so that you can create conversations with others to raise their consciousness and support them in being responsible. MADD provides numerous written materials to educate you. We are just a telephone call away.

- Be actively involved at whatever level you can. If your community has a MADD chapter, volunteer your talent and time. Explore the possibility of organizing a chapter in your community, if a local chapter does not exist. Work with other resources in your community to fight alcohol- and other drug-related driving or create resources that are missing.

Mothers Against Drunk Driving

Thank you! You have expressed a commitment to end alcohol- and other drug-related driving. For more information on MADD in your local community or how to get more involved, contact:

MADD National Office
511 E. John Carpenter Freeway, Suite 700
Irving, Texas 75062
214-744-MADD

SALADS

FOOD WRITERS' FAVORITES

EDITED BY BARBARA GIBBS OSTMANN AND JANE BAKER

ISBN 0-911479-01-5

CONTENTS

CONTRIBUTING
WRITERS

Jane Armstrong, Jane Armstrong, Inc., Oak Brook, IL
Rita Barrett, International Cookbook Services, White Plains, NY
Laura Barton, Free-Lance Writer, Portland, OR
Betty W. Bernard, *Lake Charles American Press*, Lake Charles, LA
Barbara Bloch, International Cookbook Services, White Plains, NY
Beverly Bundy, *Fort Worth Star-Telegram*, Fort Worth, TX
Barbara Burklo, (Retired) *Santa Cruz Sentinel*, Santa Cruz, CA
Toni Burks, *Roanoke Times & World-News*, Roanoke, VA
Narcisse S. Cadgène, Free-Lance Writer, New York, NY
Evelyn Cairns, *The News-Herald Newspapers*, Southgate, MI
Sally Cappon, *Santa Barbara News-Press*, Santa Barbara, CA
Leona Carlson, (Retired) *Rockford Registar Star*, Rockford, IL
Carole Currie, *Asheville Citizen*, Asheville, NC
Jeanne Delia, *The Sun News*, Myrtle Beach, SC
Louise Dodd, *Courier Herald*, Dublin, GA
Alma Drill, Free-Lance Food Writer, Bethesda, MD
Beth Whitley Duke, *Amarillo Globe-News*, Amarillo, TX
Clara Eschmann, *The Macon Telegraph and News*, Macon, GA
Carolyn Flournoy, *The Times*, Shreveport, LA
Paula M. Galusha, Free-Lance Food Writer, Tulsa, OK
Marie D. Galyean, *Idaho Press-Tribune*, Nampa, ID
June Ann Gladfelter, *The Express*, Easton, PA
Jane Witty Gould, *The Courier-News*, Bridgewater, NJ
Patricia G. Gray, *The Express*, Easton, PA
Teri M. Grimes, *The Bradenton Herald*, Bradenton, FL
Paul Grondahl, *Albany Times Union*, Albany, NY
Lorrie Guttman, *Tallahassee Democrat*, Tallahassee, FL
Suzanne Hall, *The Chattanooga Times*, Chattanooga, TN
Delia A. Hammock, *Good Housekeeping*, New York, NY
Alice Handkins, Free-Lance Food Writer, Wichita, KS
Zack Hanle, *Bon Appetit*, New York, NY
Ann Hattes, Free-Lance Food and Travel Writer, Hartland, WI

Constance Hay, Free-Lance Food Writer, Columbia, MD
Jim Hillibish, *The Repository*, Canton, OH
Monetta L. Horr, *Jackson Citizen Patriot*, Jackson, MI
Mary Beth Jung, Free-Lance Writer, Grafton, WI
Stacy Lam, *The Macon Telegraph*, Macon, GA
Lori Longbotham, Free-Lance Food Writer, New York, NY
Miriam Morgan, *San Mateo Times*, San Mateo, CA
Beth Winsten Orenstein, *The Express*, Easton, PA
Arlene Christianson Pickard, Free-Lance Food Writer, Portland, OR
John J. Poister, International News Features Network, New York, NY
Frances Price, *One and Only Cook*, Baltimore, MD
Joanna Pruess, Free-Lance Writer, New York, NY
Christine Randall, Evening Post Publishing Co., Charleston, SC
Doris Reynolds, *Naples Daily News*, Naples, FL
Delmer Robinson, *The Charleston Gazette*, Charleston, WV
Florence Roggenbach, *Norfolk Daily News*, Norfolk, NE
Susan Ruddiman, *The Mississippi Press*, Pascagoula, MS
Sally Scherer, *The Macon Telegraph*, Macon, GA
Norma Schonwetter, *Micro Magic*, Oak Park, MI
Mary D. Scourtes, *The Tampa Tribune*, Tampa, FL
Marilyn Short, Free-Lance Writer, Toronto, ONT, Canada
Virginia Shufflebarger, Free-Lance Food Writer, Alexandria, VA
Jean Smeriglio, Creative Foodworks, Granda Hills, CA
Goody L. Solomon, Free-Lance Food Writer, Washington, D.C.
Kathleen Stang, Free-Lance Writer, Seattle, WA
Caroline Stuart, *Hudson Valley Magazine*, Poughkeepsie, NY
Jeanne Voltz, Cookbook Author, Pittsboro, NC
Sue F. Wahlgren, *Herald-Leader*, Lexington, KY
Ann Corell Wells, *The Grand Rapids Press*, Grand Rapids, MI
Barbara Yost, *The Phoenix Gazette*, Phoenix, AZ

INTRODUCTION

Salads are trendy — the health foods of the '90s. Novices in the kitchen might believe that this trend is something new, but a quick look through this cookbook reveals that salads have been in style for years. Generally quick and easy to prepare, salads round out menus and add sparkle to meals.

The salad recipes in this cookbook include tried-and-true personal favorites of food writers, many regional specialties and a few gourmet treats. In many cases, the food editors and writers who contributed recipes have altered their favorites, cutting fat and calories.

The recipes have been divided into six categories: Green and vegetable salads; fruit salads; molded salads (those made with gelatin); potato, pasta and rice salads; meat, seafood and poultry salads; and salad dressings. The salad dressing category includes recipes that could be used on many different salads. Dressings recommended for specific salads are included with the salad recipes.

Each of the recipes in this cookbook includes a brief introduction that tells you something about the recipe, which makes for enjoyable reading even when you are not hungry for a salad.

These recipes are the contributors' favorites. The publisher makes no claim that the recipes are original. When possible, credit has been given where credit is due. In many cases, however, contributors have modified recipes, adding and subtracting ingredients and simplifying directions, which makes for a unique collection of recipes.

Barbara Gibbs Ostmann and Jane Baker
Editors of "Food Writers' Favorites: Salads"

About the editors:
Jane Baker is marketing coordinator for the Cherry Marketing Institute. She was food editor of The Phoenix Gazette *for 14 years and also enjoys free-lance writing and editing projects.*

Barbara Gibbs Ostmann is an assistant professor and the director of the Agricultural Journalism program at the University of Missouri-Columbia. She was food editor of the St. Louis Post-Dispatch *for 16 years, and she continues to write regularly about food and travel for several publications.*

SALAD SAVVY

Salads are easy to prepare, but a few hints can make the process go more smoothly.

- Know your greens because they are the basis of many good salads. Not only lettuce but also spinach, dandelion greens, mustard tops, watercress, chicory, radicchio or arugula can star in salads.

- Always purchase the freshest salad ingredients possible.

- The best gauge of freshness when choosing greens is how they look and smell. Choose greens that are sparkling fresh with a good color and no wilted, dry or yellowing leaves. Greens are almost all water — if they feel light, they're drying out.

- As a general rule, it is best to store greens and fresh vegetables unwashed and packed loosely in plastic bags in the refrigerator crisper drawer until shortly before use.

- Thoroughly rinse greens and vegetables in cold water just before using, then dry them on paper towels or in a salad dryer (available in the housewares department of most stores). Nothing spoils a salad faster than a bit of sand or a puddle of water in the bottom of the salad bowl.

- In preparing salads, balance textures — crunchy with soft, cooked with raw, succulent with crisp.

- Add just enough dressing to coat the salad lightly. A heavy coating of oil or mayonnaise dulls the flavors.

- You'll be ahead if you plan leftovers from other meals to work into main-course salads. Buy greens and vegetables accordingly.

- Because of the possibility of salmonella in raw eggs, it is not recommended to use raw egg yolks or whites in salads or dressings.

- Balsamic vinegar is called for in some recipes in this book. It's made from the unfermented juice of white grapes. This juice is boiled down to a sweet and intensely fruity syrup that is then aged at least six years. It has an intense sweet-tart taste. Balsamic vinegar is available at gourmet and specialty food stores and some supermarkets.

- Fruit and herb vinegars, such as raspberry vinegar or tarragon vinegar, generally are available in supermarkets.

- Rice vinegar has a sharp, clean taste that is somewhat more mellow than white vinegar. It is often used in salads with an Asian influence. Rice vinegar is generally available in supermarkets; it usually is in the aisle with Chinese or Asian foods.

- To unmold a gelatin salad, loosen the edge and around the center of ring mold with a metal spatula. For just a few seconds, dip the mold up to its rim in warm water. Tilt the mold slightly, easing the gelatin salad away from one side to let in air. Tilt and rotate the mold so that air can loosen the gelatin salad all the way around. Place a serving plate upside down over the mold. Hold the plate and mold together, then invert. Lift off the mold.

GREEN &VEGETABLE SALADS

24-Hour Vegetable Salad

Beth Winsten Orenstein
Staff Writer, *The Express*, Easton, PA

The first time I made this salad was for my sister's bridal shower. As a result, I've always thought of this salad as special-occasion fare. It requires some preparation, but I've always found the effort to be worthwhile. The peas are my favorite ingredient; they give this salad just the right zip.

Makes 8 to 10 servings

3 cups torn Romaine lettuce
Salt, to taste
Black pepper, to taste
Granulated sugar, to taste
1-1/2 cups shredded Swiss cheese, divided
4 hard-cooked eggs, peeled and sliced
1/2 pound bacon, cooked crisp and crumbled, divided

3 cups shredded iceberg lettuce
1 package (10 ounces) frozen green peas, thawed
3/4 cup mayonnaise or salad dressing
2 teaspoons sliced green onions (including some green tops)

Spread Romaine lettuce on bottom of large, clear salad bowl. Sprinkle salt, pepper and sugar on lettuce. Top with 1 cup cheese. Arrange sliced eggs on top of cheese; stand some slices on edge around inside of bowl for effect, if desired. Sprinkle generously with salt.

Make layers of half the bacon, all of the iceberg lettuce and all of the peas. Spoon mayonnaise on top; spread to cover top of salad, sealing to edge of bowl. Cover and refrigerate 24 hours.

Garnish with remaining 1/2 cup cheese, remaining half of bacon and the green onion. Toss just before serving.

Please don't drink and drive.

All-Time Antipasto Salad

Carolyn Flournoy
Food Columnist, *The Times*, Shreveport, LA

If ever there were a salad for all seasons and occasions, this is it. For many years, I have served it for our Christmas Eve party for 60 to 70 guests. It is always my choice for church suppers because it appeals to parishioners of all ages — the children can munch the carrot and celery sticks and the adults can savor the more exotic ingredients.

Makes 10 to 12 servings

2 bunches fresh broccoli (about 2 pounds)
6 carrots, pared
7 ribs celery
1 large red bell pepper
1 pound small button mushrooms
1 can (14 ounces) artichoke hearts, rinsed, drained and halved

1 can (6 ounces) pitted black olives, drained
2 cups Italian salad dressing
1 teaspoon Italian herb seasoning
2 tablespoons granulated sugar
2 teaspoons Dijon-style mustard
1 teaspoon seasoned pepper
1/4 teaspoon garlic powder

Separate broccoli into florets. Peel stems and cut into 1-inch pieces. Blanch broccoli, then refresh in cold water.

Cut carrots, celery and bell pepper into 1-1/2-inch sticks. Wipe mushrooms to clean; cut off ends of stems, if necessary.

In a large plastic container, combine broccoli, carrots, celery, bell pepper, mushrooms, artichokes and olives. Mix well.

In a blender or food processor, combine Italian salad dressing, herb seasoning, sugar, mustard, seasoned pepper and garlic power. Blend until smooth.

Pour dressing over broccoli mixture. Cover and refrigerate overnight, turning and shaking from time to time. Serve in a pretty glass or wooden bowl.

Asparagus and Tomato Salad

Alma Drill
Free-Lance Food Writer, Bethesda, MD

Most of the gourmet creations of the world pale when compared to newly picked vegetables, fresh from the garden. Dress them in something simple for a sure winner. Two of my favorite vegetables are asparagus and tomatoes. When these two vegetables are at the height of freshness, they need little to enhance them. But it's always fun to find new ways to enjoy these old favorites. This asparagus and tomato salad is served at room temperature and is a marvelous side dish with sauteed scallops or chicken. If you like, add some small cooked shrimp to the salad for a special lunch or a delicious, light supper.

Makes 4 servings

2 pounds fresh asparagus	1/4 teaspoon salt
1/3 cup plain yogurt	Dash freshly ground black pepper
1 tablespoon mayonnaise	1 cup diced tomatoes
1 tablespoon lemon juice	(about 2 medium tomatoes)

Rinse asparagus thoroughly. Gently bend each stalk until it snaps. Stalks should break where the tough ends begin; discard tough ends. Stand the stems upright in a double boiler or steamer over boiling water. Steam for 10 to 12 minutes, or until just tender. Drain thoroughly. Arrange on a platter.

In a small container, combine yogurt, mayonnaise, lemon juice, salt and pepper; mix well. Warm yogurt mixture slightly in a microwave oven or double boiler. Stir in tomatoes.

Pour yogurt-tomato mixture over asparagus. Serve salad at room temperature.

"Drunk" refers to noticeable alcohol-impaired behavior.

Broccoli Stir-Fry Slaw

Carolyn Flournoy
Food Columnist, *The Times*, Shreveport, LA

In addition to writing a weekly food column, I do a good many cooking schools and demonstrations. During the last few years, many people have asked for low-cholesterol and low-sodium recipes. When all the furor started over President George Bush and broccoli, I decided to give that vegetable a good name and answer audience requests at the same time. This broccoli slaw is low in calories, too.

Makes 6 to 8 servings

2 bunches fresh broccoli (about 2 pounds)
2 tablespoons vegetable oil
4 green onions, cut into 1-inch pieces
1 red bell pepper, cut into julienne strips
1 cup sliced fresh mushrooms

2 tablespoons white wine vinegar
2 tablespoons balsamic vinegar
2 tablespoons reduced-sodium soy sauce
1 teaspoon celery seeds
1 cup water

Trim broccoli florets; set aside. Peel broccoli stems; slice diagonally into 1/2-inch pieces. Heat oil in wok or heavy skillet. Add broccoli slices, green onions, bell pepper and mushrooms. Stir-fry about 3 minutes. Remove wok from heat. Add white wine vinegar, balsamic vinegar, soy sauce and celery seeds. Toss, then transfer mixture to a serving dish.

Add water to wok; heat to boiling. Add reserved broccoli florets; cook 2 to 3 minutes. Drain florets well, then arrange on top of cooked vegetable mixture. Serve hot or at room temperature.

Caesar Salad

Kathleen Stang
Free-Lance Writer, Seattle, WA

Caesar Salad originated in Tijuana, Mexico, in the 1920s. This make-at-the-table version is adapted from a recipe in a Sunset Magazine article years ago. I've modified the recipe, making many changes in the original. Taking current food safety concerns into consideration, I've omitted the usual raw or coddled egg; it tastes great without it.

Makes 4 to 6 servings

Croutons:
2 tablespoons olive oil
1 clove garlic, minced

2 cups cubed sourdough or French bread (1/2-inch cubes)

Dressing:
1/3 cup olive oil
2 tablespoons red wine vinegar
1 teaspoon Dijon-style mustard

1 teaspoon finely chopped anchovy fillets
1/4 teaspoon salt

Salad:
Freshly ground black pepper
1/2 lemon, wrapped in cheesecloth
1/2 cup freshly grated Parmesan cheese

1 large head Romaine lettuce, torn into large, bite-size pieces (about 7 cups)

For croutons: Heat olive oil in medium skillet over medium heat. Add garlic; sauté 2 minutes, or until golden. Add bread cubes. Cook and stir 4 minutes, or until golden brown. Remove from skillet and reserve.

For dressing: In a small jar with a tight-fitting lid, combine olive oil, vinegar, mustard, anchovies and salt. Shake well.

For salad: Place jar of dressing on a serving tray along with a pepper grinder, the lemon, Parmesan cheese and reserved croutons. Place Romaine lettuce in a large salad bowl.

At the table, grind a little pepper over Romaine; toss. Add dressing to Romaine, then squeeze lemon juice over Romaine; toss to combine. Add Parmesan cheese and croutons. Mix well. Serve immediately.

"Impaired" means a person's ability to drive safely is diminished by alcohol.

Cauliflower Salad Bowl

Christine Randall
Assistant Features Editor, Evening Post Publishing Co., Charleston, SC

This salad is one of my mother's favorites. It's tasty, easy to prepare, and great for a dinner party. It also is appropriate to take to a grieving family that has just lost a loved one. This salad is a welcome change from all the cakes, quiches and casseroles the family usually receives.

Makes 8 to 10 servings

4 cups thinly sliced cauliflower
1 cup pitted, coarsely chopped
    black olives
2/3 cup chopped green bell
    pepper
1/2 cup chopped pimento
1/2 cup chopped onion

1/2 cup vegetable oil
3 tablespoons lemon juice
3 tablespoons red or white wine
    vinegar
2 teaspoons salt
1/4 teaspoon black pepper
1/2 teaspoon granulated sugar
Lettuce leaves

In a large mixing bowl, combine cauliflower, olives, green pepper, pimento and onion. Mix well.

In another mixing bowl, combine oil, lemon juice, vinegar, salt, pepper and sugar. Mix well. Pour oil mixture over vegetable mixture. Toss to coat vegetables. Refrigerate, covered, 4 hours or overnight.

To serve, spoon vegetable mixture into a salad bowl lined with lettuce leaves.

Corn and Black Bean Salad

Jean Smeriglio
Creative Foodworks, Granada Hills, CA

I'm often asked to create something "different" for catered parties. This recipe, which was done for a barbecue party, became an instant hit. It's easy and can be made 24 hours in advance. This multi-colored salad has great eye appeal, especially when served in a terra cotta-colored bowl.

Makes 4 to 6 servings

1 can (12 ounces) whole-kernel corn, drained
1 can (15 ounces) black beans, drained and rinsed
1 red bell pepper, finely chopped
1/2 cup diagonally sliced green onions

1/2 cup chopped red onion
1 clove garlic, minced
1 medium tomato, chopped
1 jalapeño pepper, seeded and finely chopped (optional)
Cilantro sprigs or red onion wedge, for garnish

Dressing:
3/4 cup Italian salad dressing
3/4 teaspoon hot pepper sauce
1/2 teaspoon chili powder
1 tablespoon fresh lemon or lime juice

1 tablespoon chopped fresh cilantro

In a large bowl, combine corn, beans, bell pepper, green onions, red onion, garlic, tomato and jalapeño pepper.

For dressing: In a jar with a tight-fitting lid, combine Italian salad dressing, hot pepper sauce, chili powder, lemon juice and chopped cilantro. Close lid. Shake to mix well.

Pour dressing over corn mixture. Stir to mix. Refrigerate, covered, at least 6 hours, or overnight.

To serve, put corn mixture in an attractive salad bowl. Garnish with a few sprigs of cilantro or a thin wedge of red onion.

A person's ability to drive is impaired at BACs as low as .02.

Corn, Radish and Parsley Salad

Suzanne Hall
Food Editor, *The Chattanooga Times*, Chattanooga, TN

"This salad is so beautiful that I try to find special ways to serve it," says Aileen Brown, a Chattanooga herb grower. "Sometimes I hollow out tomatoes and serve the salad in them. Other times I serve it on a bed of lettuce and garnish it with tomato wedges or radish roses." A member of the Tri-State Herb Society, Brown was using herbs to season her foods long before health experts began advising all of us to do so. This is a great summertime recipe.

Makes 8 servings

4 cups fresh corn kernels
1 cup sliced radishes
1/4 cup minced fresh parsley
1/4 cup olive oil
2 tablespoons lemon juice
2 tablespoons minced fresh basil

2 tablespoons grated Parmesan cheese
1 garlic clove, minced
Salt, to taste
Black pepper, to taste

In a large saucepan, blanch the corn kernels in boiling water for 3 to 4 minutes. Drain. Rinse with cold running water to stop cooking. Drain again.

In a salad bowl, combine corn, radishes and parsley.

In a small container, combine oil, lemon juice, basil, Parmesan cheese and garlic. Pour dressing over corn mixture. Toss to coat well. Season to taste with salt and pepper. Serve at once, or refrigerate and serve chilled.

Crunchy Salad

Marilyn Short
Free-Lance Writer, Toronto, ONT, Canada

My sister, Chris Gould, invented this delicious salad several years ago. It's always a hit at parties and makes a colorful and interesting addition to a buffet table. The crunchy texture is a wonderful foil for the Oriental flavors of the dressing.

Makes 8 servings

1/4 pound snow peas
1 can (8 ounces) water chestnuts, drained, thinly sliced
2 or 3 ribs celery, sliced diagonally
2 or 3 carrots, sliced diagonally

2 red bell peppers, cut into chunks
1/2 pound fresh mushrooms, thickly sliced
Toasted slivered almonds, for garnish

Dressing:

1/2 cup peanut oil or vegetable oil
2 tablespoons red wine vinegar
1 tablespoon lemon juice

1 tablespoon soy sauce
1 tablespoon sesame seeds
Pinch granulated sugar
Black pepper, to taste

Blanch snow peas in boiling water for 10 seconds. Drain. Rinse with cold running water to stop cooking. Drain well.

In a large bowl, combine water chestnuts, celery, carrots, bell pepper, mushrooms and snow peas. Toss to combine.

For dressing: In a small bowl, combine oil, vinegar, lemon juice, soy sauce, sesame seeds, sugar and pepper. Mix well.

One hour before serving time, pour dressing over water chestnut mixture. Cover and refrigerate. Garnish with almonds right before serving.

Wait at least one hour per drink consumed before you drive.

Cucumber Dill Salad

Jane Armstrong
Jane Armstrong Inc., Oak Brook, IL

During the Chicago Symphony Orchestra's centennial tour to Russia, Budapest and Vienna, about the only fresh salad served to the group was sliced cucumbers — without any dressing. For dinner parties that followed the tour, I wanted to serve cucumbers with my CSO menu of Russian borscht, khechapuri (cheese-stuffed bread), Stroganoff, sour rye bread, Hungarian wine and Sacher torte — but I took the liberty of adding a bit of "sugar and spice" to the cucumbers.

Makes 4 servings

1/2 cup white vinegar	1/8 teaspoon white pepper
1 cup water	1 cucumber (about 1 pound)
1/2 cup granulated sugar	Chopped fresh dill
1/4 teaspoon salt	2 kiwifruit, peeled

In small saucepan, combine vinegar, water, sugar, salt and white pepper. Bring to a boil; reduce heat and simmer 1 minute, stirring to dissolve sugar.

Using thin slicing blade of food processor, slice cucumber (or, with sharp knife, cut cucumber into thin slices). Place cucumber slices in a bowl; pour vinegar mixture over cucumbers. Mix well. Add a generous sprinkling of dill. Refrigerate at least 3 hours before serving.

When ready to serve, cut kiwifruit into wedges and stir gently into cucumber mixture. Drain cucumber mixture. Serve in a glass bowl.

Danish Coleslaw

John J. Poister
Executive Editor, International News Features Network, NY, NY

The Dutch may or may not have invented coleslaw, but they did name it. The word coleslaw is derived from "cut sly," which means "chopped salad." This Danish variation is served as part of a koldebord or smorgasbord.

Makes 4 to 6 servings

4 generous cups shredded cabbage
1 small tart apple, peeled, cored and diced
4 green onions, chopped
2 tablespoons chopped fresh chives
3/4 cup dairy sour cream, lightly whipped

1/2 cup crumbled blue cheese
1/3 cup mayonnaise
2 teaspoons white wine vinegar
2 teaspoons lemon juice
1 teaspoon chopped fresh dill
Pinch paprika
Salt, to taste
Several grindings of white or black pepper

In a large mixing bowl, combine cabbage, apple, green onions, chives, sour cream, blue cheese, mayonnaise, vinegar, lemon juice and dill. Mix well. Season to taste with paprika, salt and pepper. Refrigerate, covered, several hours before serving.

Fire and Ice Tomatoes

Beverly Bundy
Food Editor, *Fort Worth Star-Telegram*, Fort Worth, TX

Best made in the summer, when tomatoes are at their natural best, this is a variation of what farm families have been eating for generations.

Makes 10 servings

6 medium tomatoes, peeled and quartered
1 medium onion, sliced
1 medium green bell pepper, cut into strips

1/4 cup water
1 tablespoon plus 2 teaspoons granulated sugar
1-1/2 teaspoons celery salt
1-1/2 teaspoons mustard seeds

1 large cucumber, peeled and sliced	1/4 teaspoon salt
3/4 cup cider vinegar	1/2 teaspoon cayenne pe
	1/8 teaspoon black pepp

In a large bowl, combine tomatoes, onion, green pepper and cucumber.

In a small saucepan, combine vinegar, water, sugar, celery salt, mustard seeds, salt, cayenne pepper and black pepper. Bring to a boil over medium-high heat; boil 1 minute. Pour hot vinegar mixture over tomato mixture. Cover and refrigerate 8 hours or overnight, to let flavors blend. Serve with a slotted spoon.

French Carrot Salad

Jane Armstrong
Jane Armstrong Inc., Oak Brook, IL

A favorite hors d'oeuvre course in France, served in the simplest to the most expensive restaurants, is marinated shredded carrots. In trying to develop something similar, I wanted to lighten it by using less oil and also give it a touch of sweetness without adding sugar. The currants and orange juice work beautifully. This makes a wonderful relish to serve with pâtés, grilled meats or sandwiches, as well as being a salad on its own.

Makes 4 to 6 servings

2 cups coarsely shredded carrots	1/4 cup vegetable oil
1/4 cup dried currants	1/8 teaspoon freshly ground
2 tablespoons lemon juice	black pepper
1/3 cup orange juice	

In a medium bowl, combine carrots, currants, lemon juice, orange juice, oil and pepper. Refrigerate several hours before serving.

acamole Salad

Teri M. Grimes
Assistant Features Editor, *The Bradenton Herald*, Bradenton, FL

Mexican food seems to get more and more popular. However, Mexican dishes often require a lot of preparation. That's why this simple Guacamole Salad is so great. Lucky for us in Florida, the main ingredients — lettuce, tomatoes and avocados — are plentiful. Just add corn chips and you have a fiesta.

Makes 6 to 8 servings

1/2 head Romaine lettuce, rinsed and drained
1/2 head iceberg lettuce, rinsed and drained
1 ripe avocado, peeled, pitted and sliced

2 medium tomatoes, cut into wedges
1/2 cup pitted, sliced black olives
1/4 cup sliced green onions
3/4 cup shredded Cheddar cheese
1 cup corn chips

Dressing:
1 ripe avocado, peeled and pitted
1 tablespoon lemon juice
1/2 cup dairy sour cream
1/3 cup vegetable oil

1 clove garlic, crushed
1/2 teaspoon granulated sugar
1/2 teaspoon chili powder
1/4 teaspoon salt
1/4 teaspoon hot pepper sauce

Line a serving bowl with Romaine leaves. Break iceberg lettuce into small pieces and add to serving bowl. Add avocado, tomatoes, olives and green onions to lettuce in bowl.

For dressing: Cut avocado into chunks. Mash avocado with an electric mixer, blender or by hand. Add lemon juice, sour cream, oil, garlic, sugar, chili powder, salt and hot pepper sauce. Blend until smooth.

Pour avocado dressing over lettuce mixture; toss to coat. Top with cheese and corn chips. Serve immediately.

Ask what police, judges and lawmakers are doing to end drunk driving.

Heavenly Carrots

Leona Carlson
Food Writer (Retired), *Rockford Register Star*, Rockford, IL

This is an old favorite. It was first discovered in the '60s, served repeatedly for years, then set aside to languish on a yellowing recipe card in my first-ever recipe file, where I rediscovered it in 1990. It's as much of a hit as ever the second time around. Technically, it's a side dish, suitable for serving in place of a salad. Similar recipes often go by the name, Copper Pennies.

Makes 16 servings

2 pounds carrots	1/2 cup vegetable oil
1 small green bell pepper, thinly sliced	1 cup granulated sugar
	3/4 cup white vinegar
1 medium onion, thinly sliced	1 teaspoon prepared mustard
1 can (10-1/2 ounces) condensed cream of tomato soup, undiluted	1 teaspoon Worcestershire sauce
	Salt, to taste

Pare carrots; cut into rounds or on the diagonal. Boil carrots in salted water just until tender-crisp. Drain. Arrange carrots, green pepper and onion in layers in a flat pan or bowl.

In a small mixing bowl, combine tomato soup, oil, sugar, vinegar, mustard and Worcestershire sauce. Mix well. Season to taste with salt. Pour sauce over vegetables. Refrigerate overnight before serving.

Note: This salad keeps for three to four days in the refrigerator.

Mediterranean Tomato Salad

Leona Carlson
Food Writer (Retired), *Rockford Register Star*, Rockford, IL

This salad is the ultimate complement to moussaka, meatballs, lamb or whatever you choose to serve at a Greek dinner party. The tomatoes, olives and cheese furnish dramatic color. The herbs and vinegar lend Mediterranean flavor. Oopah! Zorba would love it.

Makes 6 servings

1 clove garlic	1/2 cup olive oil
3 large, ripe tomatoes, cut into bite-sized pieces	1/2 teaspoon dried oregano
	1/2 teaspoon dried thyme
12 pitted black olives, halved	Salt, to taste
3/4 cup cubed Feta cheese	Freshly ground black pepper, to taste
3 tablespoons red wine vinegar	

Halve garlic; rub a large salad bowl with cut side of garlic. Discard garlic. Combine tomatoes, olives and cheese in salad bowl. Add vinegar, oil, oregano and thyme; toss to mix well. Season with salt and pepper.

Cover and refrigerate at least 4 hours, to let flavors blend. Let salad stand at room temperature 1 or 2 hours before serving.

Note: If desired, drain some of the dressing before serving. Thoroughly drain leftovers before storing in the refrigerator.

Vote for tougher drunk driving laws.

Mock Lobster Salad

Free-Lance Food and Travel Writer, Hartland, WI

Free-Lance Food and Travel Writer, Hartland, WI

This recipe was given to me by a college friend from the South who got it from her mother. I have never run across a similar recipe, so it might have been unique to my friend's family. I especially enjoy making this salad when I have loads of fresh garden tomatoes. The taste and consistency vary with the tomatoes used, as well as the choice of crackers used for the crumbs. That makes this recipe especially delightful for the cook who likes to improvise and vary the ingredients. Although I have listed amounts for the cracker crumbs and mayonnaise, these should be considered suggestions only, to be modified to suit your taste and preference. When the fresh tomatoes are quite juicy, the salad will absorb more cracker crumbs. Even the amount of onion and celery can be varied according to taste. This salad is a tasty, healthful and economical summer salad, although I doubt anyone will really think it is lobster.

Makes 4 to 5 servings

2 pounds fresh tomatoes
   (fresh tomatoes are preferred,
   but you can substitute two
   16-ounce cans tomatoes)
1 green bell pepper, finely
   chopped
4 ribs celery, chopped
1/2 medium onion, finely chopped

1-1/2 cups cracker crumbs
1 to 1-1/2 tablespoons
   mayonnaise
2 hard-cooked eggs, peeled
   and chopped
Leaf lettuce, rinsed and well
   drained

Rinse tomatoes; chop into small pieces. (If using canned tomatoes, drain, then mash or chop them.) Add green pepper, celery and onion to tomatoes.

Add enough cracker crumbs to absorb tomato juice. (With juicy tomatoes, it is quite possible you'll need more than 1-1/2 cups crumbs.)

Add 1 tablespoon mayonnaise to tomato mixture. Mix well. Add remaining 1/2 tablespoon mayonnaise, if needed to give salad desired consistency.

Add eggs; toss lightly. Refrigerate until well chilled. Serve on lettuce leaves.

Send "thank you" letters to legislators who sponsor stronger drunk driving laws.   33

Mushroom and Green Bean Salad

Barbara Burklo
Food Editor (Retired), *Santa Cruz Sentinel*, Santa Cruz, CA

Mushrooms are a major crop in the Santa Cruz area. We can purchase them here at their plump, fresh best. This make-ahead salad combines mushrooms with green beans and red pepper for a colorful, flavorful salad.

Makes 4 servings

3/4 pound fresh green beans, trimmed
2 tablespoons minced shallots
1/4 cup mayonnaise
3 tablespoons fresh lemon juice
2 tablespoons vegetable or olive oil

1 tablespoon Dijon-style mustard
2 cups sliced fresh mushrooms
1/4 cup chopped red bell pepper
1 tablespoon minced fresh basil or 3/4 teaspoon dried basil
Freshly ground black pepper
Tomato wedges, for garnish

Cut beans into 1-1/2-inch lengths. Cover with water and cook on top of the stove, or add 3 tablespoons water and cook in a microwave oven, just until beans are crisp-tender. Do not overcook. Drain beans. Cover with ice water to stop cooking; set aside.

In a small bowl, combine shallots, mayonnaise, lemon juice, oil and mustard; mix well.

Drain beans; pour shallot mixture over beans. Add mushrooms, bell pepper and basil. Toss to coat vegetables. Cover and refrigerate several hours.

At serving time, season to taste with pepper and garnish with tomato wedges.

Note: Frozen green beans can be used instead of fresh. Cook quickly, chill, then proceed as directed.

Send a "letter to the editor" expressing your support for stronger drunk driving legislation.

Northwest Spinach Salad

Laura Barton
Free-Lance Writer, Portland, OR

Spinach has always been a favorite in our family. When I moved to the Northwest, I quickly adapted this version of spinach salad to use readily available hazelnuts. If hazelnuts (filberts) are not available, try adding toasted walnuts or pine nuts because they also add a delicious flavor. But the hazelnuts are my first choice!

Makes 6 servings

1 bunch fresh spinach, rinsed
   and torn into bite-size pieces
1-1/2 cups sliced fresh mushrooms
1/4 cup crumbled mild blue cheese
2 green onions, chopped

1/2 cup toasted hazelnuts
Raspberry vinaigrette
   (or favorite vinaigrette
   dressing)

In a medium bowl, combine spinach, mushrooms, blue cheese, green onions and hazelnuts. Mix well. Just before serving, pour vinaigrette over spinach mixture. Toss to coat well.

Okra Salad

Sally Scherer
Food Writer, *The Macon Telegraph*, Macon, GA

When I moved to Georgia 12 years ago, I had never heard of okra. The first few times I tried okra, I was sorry I had ever heard of it! But at a recent family-night supper at my church, this salad appeared. I tried it. I liked it. With garden-grown tomatoes and a sweet Vidalia onion, Okra Salad is a real hit!

Makes 4 servings

8 slices bacon
1-1/2 pounds fresh okra
1 cup yellow cornmeal
1 tablespoon all-purpose flour
1/2 teaspoon salt

1 fresh tomato, chopped
1 medium onion, finely chopped
1/2 teaspoon salt
1/4 teaspoon black pepper

Fry bacon in a heavy skillet until crisp. Drain on paper towels. Crumble bacon and set aside. Reserve drippings in skillet.

Rinse okra in cold water; drain on paper towels. Cut off tip and stem ends, then cut okra crosswise into 1/2-inch slices.

Sift together cornmeal, flour and salt. Roll okra in cornmeal mixture. Sauté okra in reserved bacon drippings until golden brown. Drain on paper towels.

In a large salad bowl, combine okra, tomato and onion; add salt, pepper and reserved crumbled bacon. Toss lightly. Serve at once.

Support Sobriety Checkpoints. They stop drunk drivers and save lives.

Oriental Salad

Louise Dodd
Food Editor, *Courier Herald*, Dublin, GA

You wouldn't think a college beauty queen who later became the mother of five children and served in the Georgia House of Representatives would also be an outstanding cook. Such are the qualities of one of my college roommates, Mary Ida. At a reunion luncheon one day, she served this different-tasting salad that sent all the guests scurrying for pens and paper so they could write down the recipe for future use.

Makes 6 to 8 servings

1 can (14 to 16 ounces) bean sprouts, drained

1 can (8 ounces) bamboo shoots, drained

1 can (8 ounces) sliced water chestnuts, drained

1 jar (4 ounces) chopped pimentos, drained

1 can (11 ounces) mandarin oranges, drained

1 medium onion, thinly sliced

1/2 cup finely chopped celery

1/2 cup finely chopped green bell pepper

1/3 cup vegetable oil

3/4 cup granulated sugar

2/3 cup white vinegar

1 teaspoon salt

1 teaspoon black pepper

In a large salad bowl, combine bean sprouts, bamboo shoots, water chestnuts, pimentos, mandarin oranges, onion, celery and green pepper.

In a small saucepan, combine oil, sugar, vinegar, salt and pepper. Cook over medium-high heat until mixture boils and sugar is dissolved. Remove from heat and carefully pour hot oil mixture over vegetable mixture. Refrigerate until chilled.

Radish Salad

Lori Longbotham
Free-Lance Food Writer, New York, NY

This salad is perfect for a summer luncheon or dinner. It's healthful, pretty and unusual. You might even try using it as a topping for chilled poached chicken breasts or for chilled poached fish steaks or fillets — salmon would be wonderful. Give it a try. Radishes are too delicious to be used just for garnishes on relish trays.

Makes 2 servings

1 tablespoon fresh orange juice
2 teaspoons fresh lemon juice
1 teaspoon olive oil
1 teaspoon orange flower water
(available at specialty stores
and some supermarkets)

Pinch salt
Pinch cayenne pepper
1-1/2 cups thinly sliced radishes
1/2 cup peeled, seeded and thinly
sliced cucumber
Mint sprigs, for garnish (optional)

In a medium bowl, combine orange juice, lemon juice, oil, orange flower water, salt and cayenne. Stir in radishes and cucumber. Toss to coat vegetables. Garnish with mint sprigs, if desired. Serve immediately.

Please say "crash" — not "accident" — when talking about alcohol-related collisions.

Romaine and Artichoke Salad

Mary Beth Jung
Free-Lance Writer, Grafton, WI

Here's a salad recipe that has delighted many a dinner guest at my home. It was given to me by a friend who enjoyed this salad at a restaurant in St. Louis. For a crowd, it can be doubled or tripled. For real convenience, I prepare and chill the greens and assemble the dressing hours before my company arrives. Then it is easy to simply toss and serve this pretty salad.

Makes 6 servings

1 head iceberg lettuce, shredded or torn
1 quart shredded or torn Romaine lettuce
1 small red onion, thinly sliced
1 can (14 ounces) artichoke hearts, rinsed, drained and quartered
1 jar (2 ounces) chopped pimento, drained

2/3 cup olive oil
1/3 cup red wine vinegar
Salt, to taste
Freshly ground black pepper, to taste
3/4 cup grated Parmesan cheese

In a salad bowl, combine iceberg and Romaine lettuces, onion, artichoke hearts and pimento. Toss to mix.

In a measuring cup or small mixing bowl, combine oil, vinegar, salt and pepper. Pour over lettuce mixture. Toss to coat all ingredients well. Add cheese; toss again. Serve immediately.

Snow Pea Salad

Suzanne Hall
Food Editor, *The Chattanooga Times*, Chattanooga, TN

I first met Chattanooga attorney Eron Epstein on a story assignment. He's a fine and imaginative cook who soon became a good friend. "I love to read cookbooks and am always on the lookout for unusual ones," he says. "But I change just about all the recipes I use. I like to add my own touch." A native of Chattanooga, Epstein loves to travel and sample different kinds of food. At home, he often combines foods from many countries into one menu. This salad is especially good with grilled chicken or fish.

Makes 6 to 8 servings

2 cups snow peas
2 large red or green bell peppers,
     sliced into rings
1/2 pound fresh mushrooms,
     sliced
1/3 cup walnut oil (available
     in specialty shops and
     some supermarkets)

2 tablespoons champagne
     vinegar or white wine vinegar
1 tablespoon granulated sugar
1 tablespoon lemon juice
Toasted sesame seeds

Blanch snow peas 1 to 2 minutes. Drain. Rinse with cold running water to stop cooking. Let cool.

In a large glass bowl, combine snow peas, pepper rings and mushrooms.

In a small container, combine oil, vinegar, sugar and lemon juice.

Just before serving, toss vegetable mixture with oil mixture. Sprinkle sesame seeds on top.

Please don't laugh at or tell stories that treat drunk driving humorously.

Spinach Salad

Norma Schonwetter
Syndicated Columnist, *Micro Magic*, Oak Park, MI

I've always loved spinach, especially in a salad. I found a good recipe many years ago in a newspaper, then modified it to reduce the saturated fat, sodium and calories. It became a family favorite for a lunch main dish or as a side salad for dinner. Sometimes I omit the bacon or substitute imitation bacon bits. You can cook the bacon and heat the dressing in a microwave oven, if you prefer.

Makes 6 servings

6 slices bacon
2 quarts torn spinach, stems
    removed (one 10-ounce
    package fresh spinach)
1/2 cup chopped onion
1 cup halved cherry tomatoes
1/2 teaspoon low-sodium
    Worcestershire sauce

1 tablespoon granulated sugar or
    low-calorie sugar substitute
1/2 teaspoon salt (optional)
1/4 teaspoon dry mustard
2 tablespoons lemon juice
1 tablespoon ketchup
3 tablespoons olive oil

Cook bacon in skillet until crisp. Drain well on paper towels. Crumble and set aside.

In a large salad bowl, combine spinach, onion and cherry tomatoes.

In small saucepan, combine Worcestershire sauce, sugar, salt, dry mustard, lemon juice, ketchup and oil. Cook over medium heat until sugar dissolves and mixture is bubbly.

Pour hot dressing over spinach mixture. Add reserved crumbled bacon and toss well. Serve immediately.

Spinach with Sesame Dressing

Jane Witty Gould
Lifestyle Copy Editor, *The Courier-News*, Bridgewater, NJ

My search for low-cholesterol food led me straight to Japanese cuisine. Beyond sushi and sashimi, I discovered a world of easy, tasty vegetables and salads. This salad was inspired by an article about Japanese spring cookery by Elizabeth Andoh. Over the years, I have changed the recipe, adding oil, decreasing the amount of sugar, and using reduced-sodium soy sauce.

Makes 6 servings

1 pound fresh spinach, rinsed and trimmed
3 tablespoons sesame seeds
1-1/2 tablespoons superfine granulated sugar

2 tablespoons reduced-sodium soy sauce
1 teaspoon vegetable oil

Plunge the spinach into a large pot of boiling, salted water; cook for barely a minute, or until leaves wilt and turn bright green. Drain immediately; refresh in a colander under cold running water. Squeeze liquid out of the spinach, a handful at a time. Cut dry handfuls of spinach into 1/2-inch slices; place in a bowl. Set aside.

Roast sesame seeds over medium heat in a small, heavy skillet, shaking the pan so the seeds do not burn. Transfer the sesame seeds to a mini-food processor and process until they become pasty. (Traditionally, this is done in a Japanese mortar called a *suribachi*, but an inexpensive Mexican *molcajete* made from black basalt will do, as will a mini-food processor, small electric chopper or hand-held nut grinder.)

Transfer ground sesame seeds to a small bowl. Add sugar, soy sauce and oil; mix well. Pour sesame seed mixture over spinach; toss gently. The salad can be refrigerated, covered, for up to two hours. Return to room temperature before serving.

2,662 teenagers between 15 and 19 were killed in alcohol-related crashes in 1990.

Surprise Salad

Christine Randall
Assistant Features Editor, Evening Post Publishing Co., Charleston, SC

My mother received this recipe from a friend. The friend, who now is in a nursing home, didn't cook much, but this salad was one of her specialties. It might sound a little weird, but it is delicious.

Makes 10 servings

2 cups well-drained sauerkraut
2 cups shredded carrots
1 cup finely chopped celery
1 cup finely chopped green
    bell pepper
1/2 cup chopped onion

1/4 cup chopped pimento
1/2 cup granulated sugar
1/3 cup white vinegar
1 teaspoon salt
Dash black pepper

In a large mixing bowl, combine sauerkraut, carrots, celery, green pepper, onion and pimento.

In a separate bowl, combine sugar, vinegar, salt and pepper; pour over sauerkraut mixture. Toss to mix. Refrigerate, covered, at least 4 hours before serving.

Note: This salad can be refrigerated up to one week before serving.

Sweet Onion Salad

Frances Price
Columnist, *One and Only Cook*, Baltimore, MD

Being an onion aficionado, I ordered insalada of Vidalia, the salad du jour at Scoozi, one of Chicago's most popular restaurants. I was not disappointed with my salad selection. Three each of the thinnest slices of red-ripe tomato and Vidalia onion, perfectly matched in size, were fanned alternately across a plate innocent of lettuce. With crusty French bread, a double helping of this salad makes a sumptuous supper for one.

Makes 2 servings

1/2 large Vidalia or other sweet onion, thinly sliced

1 large red ripe tomato, thinly sliced

2 teaspoons olive oil

2 teaspoons red wine vinegar

2 to 3 leaves fresh basil, thinly sliced, or 1/2 teaspoon dried basil

2 ounces feta or goat cheese, crumbled

French bread

Artistically arrange equal portions of onion and tomato slices on two dinner plates. Drizzle oil, then vinegar on each salad. Sprinkle basil, then cheese over each. Serve with warm French bread.

Thai Eggplant Salad

Lori Longbotham
Free-Lance Food Writer, New York, NY

Thai food is one of the most popular ethnic cuisines these days— and no wonder. It has exciting flavors, is easy to prepare, and is almost always low in calories. This dish, for example, has only 33 calories per serving. As an added bonus, this dish is low in fat, so you can serve it and encourage your friends and family to enjoy it in good health.

Makes 10 servings

2 medium eggplants
  (about 12 ounces each)
2 shallots, finely chopped
2 cloves garlic, finely chopped
2 tablespoons finely chopped fresh
  cilantro
1/2 to 1 teaspoon crushed hot red
  pepper flakes

1/4 cup fish sauce (see note)
1/4 cup fresh lemon juice
  (about 1 lemon)
2 tablespoons fresh lime juice
  (about 1 lime)
1/2 teaspoon grated lemon peel
1/2 teaspoon grated lime peel
2 green onions, finely chopped

Peel eggplants; cut into 2 x 3/4 x 3/4-inch strips. Steam in a colander or vegetable steamer over boiling water 7 to 10 minutes, or until tender. Let cool to room temperature.

Place shallots, garlic, cilantro and red pepper flakes on a cutting board. Mince, then mash to a paste with the side of a chef's knife.

In a large mixing bowl, combine cooled eggplant strips, shallot mixture, fish sauce, lemon juice, lime juice, lemon peel and lime peel. Let stand at room temperature 20 minutes to allow flavors to blend. Transfer to serving dish, garnish with green onions, and serve at room temperature.

Note: Fish sauce, called "nam pla" by the Thai and "nuoc mam" by the Vietnamese, is available at Oriental groceries and in the international section of some supermarkets.

Turnip Salad

Betty W. Bernard
Food Editor, *Lake Charles American Press*, Lake Charles, LA

In southwest Louisiana, where there are few hard freezes in winter, home gardeners can enjoy a variety of fresh vegetables all year long. Underground root crops, such as turnips and carrots, are almost always available, even in the coldest weather. Even children who turn up their noses at cooked turnips — or cooked carrots — often enjoy eating them raw. It is easy to incorporate nutritious vegetables into the diet with fresh salads such as this one.

Makes 4 servings

2 medium turnips	1/2 teaspoon salt
1 small carrot	1/2 teaspoon granulated sugar
1 small apple	Pinch cayenne pepper (optional)
1/2 cup seedless raisins	Mayonnaise

Rinse turnips and carrot. Cut off and discard any stem portions. Drain on paper towels to absorb excess moisture. Core the apple, but do not peel.

Use a food chopper, food processor or grater to shred turnips, carrot and apple.

In a medium mixing bowl, combine turnips, carrot, apple, raisins, salt, sugar and cayenne. Stir lightly with a fork to distribute evenly. Add mayonnaise in small amounts, blending in just until mixture will hold together. Refrigerate before serving.

Wilted Lettuce

Toni Burks
Food Editor, *Roanoke Times & World-News*, Roanoke, VA

My grandmother had several spring rituals. One was brewing sassafras tea, which cures just about anything that might ail you. Another was making wilted lettuce salad — scalded salad, she called it. Quite simply, it consists of lots of tender lettuce leaves, some tender green onions and just enough hot bacon dressing to wilt it down to about half its original quantity. It's a great way to welcome spring.

Makes 6 servings

4 to 5 slices bacon	6 slender green onions, chopped
5 to 6 cups packed torn leaf lettuce	1/4 cup buttermilk

Cook bacon in skillet until crisp. Drain on paper towels. Crumble bacon; reserve. Reserve 1/4 cup drippings in skillet.

Combine lettuce and green onions in a warmed serving bowl.

Heat reserved 1/4 cup bacon drippings over medium-high heat until quite hot. Remove from heat and immediately add buttermilk. Swirl around in pan to mix.

Immediately pour hot dressing over lettuce mixture; toss to blend. Sprinkle reserved crumbled bacon on salad. Serve at once.

Note: You can substitute 1/4 cup cider vinegar or lemon juice for the buttermilk, but the flavor will be compromised.

Zucchini Salad, Italian Style

Zack Hanle
Editor-at-large, *Bon Appetit*, New York, NY

> *An Italian friend of mine, Katie Trotta, gave me this recipe. The mint leaves add a different flavor to the zucchini. It's the perfect pairing of two abundant summer treats from the garden.*

Makes 6 servings

6 cucumber-size zucchini
1 large onion, finely chopped
1/2 cup finely chopped, tightly
    packed fresh mint leaves
3/4 cup fine dry bread crumbs

Salt, to taste
Black pepper, to taste
3/4 cup French salad dressing
Lettuce leaves
6 small mint sprigs, for garnish

Trim ends of zucchini; cut zucchini crosswise into 3/4-inch rounds. Put zucchini in a large saucepan and cover with water. Cook over high heat 5 to 7 minutes, or until zucchini is barely tender. Drain and let cool.

Place one-third of the cooked zucchini in a 2-quart casserole dish. Add a layer of one-third of the onions, then one-third of the mint and one-third of the bread crumbs. Repeat layers of zucchini, onions, mint and bread crumbs until all ingredients are used (three layers of each ingredient, ending with bread crumbs). Season with salt and pepper. Pour French dressing over the top. Cover with a plate and a weight. Refrigerate several hours, or until thoroughly chilled. Serve on lettuce leaves and garnish with mint sprigs.

Note: This salad keeps for several days in the refrigerator. The flavor improves with age.

FRUIT SALADS

California Salad Tray with Honey-Roasted Almonds

Barbara Burklo
Food Editor (Retired), *Santa Cruz Sentinel*, Santa Cruz, CA

> *Californians love fresh fruit, and because we are blessed with such an abundance of fruit, we find lots of ways to use it all. This fresh fruit salad tray can contain whatever fruits are in season. The Honey-Roasted Almonds accompanying it are wonderful with any fruit. Serve crusty bread with the salad tray.*

Makes 4 to 6 servings

Honey-Roasted Almonds:
2 cups whole almonds
2 tablespoons soy sauce
2 tablespoons honey
1/2 teaspoon grated orange peel
1/2 teaspoon garlic powder
1/2 teaspoon ground ginger
2 teaspoons almond oil or
    vegetable oil

Salad Tray:
1 head Romaine lettuce, rinsed
    and drained
Melon wedges (melon of choice;
    one or several kinds)
Fresh strawberries, rinsed
    and hulled
Fresh pineapple wedges
Seedless grapes, rinsed and
    drained
Assorted wedges of cheese
    (caraway, hot pepper
    or a variety)

For almonds: Spread almonds in a shallow pan. Toast in a preheated 350-degree oven 15 minutes, stirring once or twice. Let cool. Reduce oven temperature to 250 degrees.

In a small saucepan, blend soy sauce with honey. Stir in orange peel, garlic powder and ginger. Bring mixture to a boil over medium heat. Stir in almonds; toss to coat evenly. Boil, stirring constantly, 5 minutes, or until liquid is absorbed. Add oil and toss.

Place almonds in a single layer on a baking sheet, separating almonds. Bake in center of a preheated 250-degree oven 15 minutes. Pour out onto oiled aluminum foil or other non-stick surface. Toss and separate every 5 minutes until cool. Store cooled almonds in tightly closed plastic bag. Almonds can be frozen for later use.

Help plan an alcohol-free prom/graduation party.

For salad tray: On a tray or platter, arrange lettuce leaves. In layered rows, arrange melon, strawberries, pineapple and grapes. Tuck cheese wedges around edges. At end or side of platter, place Honey-Roasted Almonds.

Christmas Cranberry Salad

Beverly Bundy
Food Editor, *Fort Worth Star-Telegram*, Fort Worth, TX

My mother-in-law made this salad every Christmas for her family. Although our holiday menus tend to be more adventuresome these days, my husband doesn't think it's Christmas unless I include this salad.

Makes 8 servings

2 cups ground cranberries (grind fresh or frozen cranberries in food processor or blender)
3 cups miniature marshmallows
3/4 cup granulated sugar

2 cups diced Granny Smith apples (unpeeled)
1/2 cup halved seedless grapes
1/2 cup chopped pecans
1 cup heavy cream, whipped

In a mixing bowl, combine cranberries, marshmallows and sugar. Refrigerate overnight.

Add apples, grapes and pecans to cranberry mixture; mix well. Fold in whipped cream. Serve immediately. This colorful salad is pretty served in a glass bowl.

Cranberry Delight Salad

Sue F. Wahlgren
Columnist, *Lexington Herald-Leader*, Lexington, KY

I discovered this recipe about 10 years ago when I was working late at the office. It was during the Christmas holidays and I was having 10 guests for a holiday dinner. A fellow worker heard me saying that as much of the meal as possible had to be prepared ahead of time, so she volunteered this salad recipe.

It was one of the special dishes of the meal, and I have been making it ever since. Once you have prepared it, Cranberry Delight can be stuck in the freezer and forgotten until serving time.

Makes 10 to 12 servings

1 package (8 ounces) cream cheese, softened
2 tablespoons mayonnaise (either regular or light)
2 tablespoons granulated sugar
1 can (16 ounces) whole-berry cranberry sauce
1 can (8 ounces) crushed pineapple
3/4 cup chopped pecans
1 cup heavy cream, whipped

In a large mixing bowl, combine cream cheese, mayonnaise and sugar; mix well. Stir in cranberry sauce, pineapple with its juice, and pecans. Fold in whipped cream. Pour mixture into an 8x8x2-inch pan. Freeze until firm. Let thaw 5 minutes before serving.

Tell your legislators that you endorse a .00 BAC for drivers under 21.

Dixie Cup Salad

Beth Whitley Duke
Food Editor, *Amarillo Globe-News*, Amarillo, TX

Almost every cook has a favorite frozen fruit salad recipe. I call this one Dixie Cup Salad — not for a Southern tradition, but because the easiest way to make it is to use that old kitchen standby, Dixie Cups. By freezing the salad in four- or six-ounce paper cups, you create individual-size servings in molded shapes. Rather than having to turn the salad out of a greased mold, you simply peel the paper away from the frozen mixture and discard the paper.

Makes 8 servings

2 cups dairy sour cream
2 tablespoons lemon juice
3/4 cup granulated sugar
1/8 teaspoon salt
1 can (8 ounces) crushed
   pineapple, drained

1/2 cup chopped maraschino
   cherries
1/4 cup chopped pecans
1 banana, peeled and sliced
1/2 cup miniature marshmallows

In a mixing bowl, combine sour cream, lemon juice, sugar and salt. Stir in pineapple, cherries, pecans, banana and marshmallows. Spoon into eight (4-ounce) paper cups. Freeze until firm. Let thaw for several minutes before serving.

Note: If you have the ingredients on hand, double the recipe and store the extra cups in the freezer for a quick salad, snack or dessert.

Ensalada de Nochebuena (Christmas Eve Salad)

Kathleen Stang
Free-Lance Writer, Seattle, WA

Christmas Eve Salad is traditionally served on December 24 in Mexico, but I find it goes well throughout the holiday season. Arrange the colorful fruit with the sliced beets and jicama in a shallow glass bowl or platter. Serve it buffet style, adding the vinaigrette dressing at the last minute.

Makes 8 servings

1 large head Romaine lettuce
1 can (16 ounces) small beets, drained and sliced
3 oranges, peeled and thinly sliced
2 bananas, peeled and thinly sliced
1 small pineapple, peeled, cored and cut into chunks (or one 16-ounce can pineapple chunks, drained)

1 cup sliced jicama (optional)
1 lime, peeled and sliced thin
1/2 cup pomegranate seeds (optional)
1/2 cup chopped peanuts
1/2 cup vegetable oil
1/4 cup red wine vinegar
1/4 teaspoon salt
Dash cayenne pepper

Remove large outer leaves from Romaine; rinse and drain. Use these leaves to line a large, shallow salad bowl. Rinse and drain remaining Romaine; coarsely shred and place in salad bowl. Attractively arrange beets, oranges, bananas, pineapple and jicama on top of shredded lettuce. Garnish salad with lime slices, pomegranate seeds and peanuts.

In a small bowl, combine oil, vinegar, salt and cayenne. Pour dressing over salad just before serving.

Don't let others teach youngsters the wrong lessons about alcohol.

Fennel-Apple-Camembert Salad

Barbara Bloch
President, International Cookbook Services, White Plains, NY

I love the French custom of serving cheese and bread between the main course and dessert. But with so many people watching cholesterol and calories, it no longer seems a sensible thing to serve. This salad is a great alternative — the refreshing licorice flavor of fennel combines nicely with the apples and cheese.

Makes 4 to 6 servings

2 medium fennel bulbs
3 firm apples, cored, thinly
    sliced and sprinkled with
    lemon juice
1/4 pound Camembert cheese,
    rind removed, cubed
1/2 cup coarsely chopped nuts
    (almonds, hazelnuts
    or pecans)

1/2 cup mayonnaise
5 tablespoons orange juice
Salt, to taste
Freshly ground black pepper,
    to taste

Cut fennel bulbs in half lengthwise. Trim green feathery leaves; reserve leaves for garnish. Thinly slice fennel; place slices in serving bowl. Add apple slices, cheese cubes and nuts.

In a small bowl, combine mayonnaise, orange juice, salt and pepper. Spoon over salad; toss to coat.

Cover and refrigerate salad until serving time. Garnish salad with reserved fennel leaves. Serve salad between the main course and dessert.

Fruit Salad with Mint Ricotta Whip

Lori Longbotham
Free-Lance Food Writer, New York, NY

Ricotta cheese is so often overlooked, and it's a shame. When you're watching fats and calories, nothing is as smooth and creamy as blended light or part-skim ricotta. You might want to try blending in some spices, such as cinnamon or nutmeg.

Makes 2 servings

1 ripe peach, pared, seeded and diced
1/2 papaya, pared, seeded and diced
10 strawberries, hulled and sliced
2/3 cup diced honeydew melon
2/3 cup diced cantaloupe
2/3 cup diced fresh pineapple

1/3 cup fresh raspberries
2/3 cup light or part-skim ricotta cheese
2 tablespoons minced fresh mint
2 to 3 tablespoons fresh lime juice
1 teaspoon superfine granulated sugar
Mint sprigs, for garnish

In a large mixing bowl, combine peach, papaya, strawberries, honeydew, cantaloupe, pineapple and raspberries.

Purée ricotta cheese in food processor or blender 2 minutes, or until smooth. Transfer to a small bowl. Stir in mint, lime juice and sugar.

Spoon fruit mixture into two salad bowls; top with ricotta mixture. Garnish with mint sprigs. Serve at once.

Grapefruit-Avocado Salad with Orange-Cumin Dressing

Jeanne Voltz
Cookbook Author, Pittsboro, NC

Grapefruit and avocado have been going steady since the first cook in Florida got creative. It's a good partnership, but boring. Perk up the dressing with cumin and scatter a few Mediterranean olives around, and you and your guests won't find it boring at all. We serve this as a hearty side-dish to cold roast chicken or grilled steaks.

Tell young people about the dangers of drinking and driving.

Makes 4 servings

2 large grapefruits
2 ripe avocados
2 red onions, sliced thin and
    separated into rings
1/2 teaspoon salt
1/4 teaspoon freshly ground
    black pepper

1 or 2 bunches arugula, salad
    savoy or leaf lettuce, rinsed
    and drained
10 or 12 Mediterranean black
    olives

Orange-Cumin Dressing:
2 tablespoons lemon juice
1/4 cup orange juice
2 teaspoons ground cumin
1 clove garlic, minced
1/2 teaspoon salt

1/8 teaspoon freshly ground
    black pepper
2 or 3 dashes hot pepper sauce
1/2 cup olive oil

Peel grapefruits by cutting from top to bottom with a sharp knife on a cutting board. Peel off every last trace of white pith. Holding fruit over a bowl, section it by cutting from outside to core, then out again, loosening each section. Place grapefruit sections on a plate, but reserve juice in bowl.

Peel and thinly slice avocados. Add avocado slices to reserved grapefruit juice in bowl; toss lightly to coat well. (If not coated, squeeze grapefruit cores over avocado.) Add onion rings; coat with grapefruit juice. Add salt and pepper.

For dressing: In a bowl or jar with a tight-fitting lid, combine lemon juice, orange juice, cumin, garlic, salt, pepper and hot pepper sauce. Whisk or shake until well mixed. Add olive oil; whisk or shake until blended. Whisk or shake again just before serving.

To assemble salad, arrange greens around outer edge of platter or on individual salad plates. Arrange grapefruit sections and avocado slices in center. Garnish with onion rings and olives. Drizzle a few tablespoons of dressing over salad and pass remainder of dressing at table.

Hawaiian Salad with Mango Dressing

Barbara Yost
Feature Writer, *The Phoenix Gazette*, Phoenix, AZ

When I was in Kauai, Hawaii, several years ago, I stayed at a hotel that served the most lavish Sunday brunch I've ever seen. People came from all over the island and stood in line for hours for this fabulous buffet. Of all the food stations, the fresh fruit table was the best and the prettiest. This salad reminds me of that beautiful brunch and the tropical fruits served there. I can't go to Hawaii every Sunday, but I can have a little taste of it whenever I want.

Makes 8 servings

Dressing:

1 medium-size ripe mango
2 tablespoons lemon juice
2 tablespoons lime juice
Salt, to taste
Freshly ground black pepper, to taste
3/4 cup vegetable oil

Salad:

Red leaf lettuce
2 medium papayas, peeled and quartered
2 large ripe avocados, peeled and quartered
1 small red onion, sliced very thin
2 kiwifruit, peeled and cut into 4 slices each
Shredded coconut

For the dressing: Roll unpeeled mango on countertop to soften. Cut off one end and squeeze juice into a small bowl. Add lemon juice, lime juice, salt and pepper to mango juice. Whisk in oil, a little at a time. Let stand at room temperature one hour.

For the salad: Arrange a nest of lettuce leaves on each of eight salad plates. Thinly slice papaya and avocado quarters. Arrange papaya and avocado slices on top of lettuce. Arrange three onion rings and a slice of kiwifruit on each salad. Top each with a sprinkling of coconut. Spoon dressing over salads just before serving.

Never serve alcohol to anyone under the age of 21.

Mandarin Orange and Onion Salad

Doris Reynolds
Food Columnist, *Naples Daily News*, Naples, FL

This salad came about when I had unexpected guests. Because I always keep a can of mandarin oranges on my shelf, I decided to combine it with onions. It was a big hit. Over the years I have made variations that are equally delicious. Marinating the oranges and onions ahead of time enhances the flavor. This is a great salad to serve with pasta and meat sauce — a welcome change from tossed greens.

Makes 4 to 6 servings

1 can (11 ounces) mandarin
   oranges, drained
1 medium-size red onion, cut into
   thin slices
2 tablespoons poppy seeds
3 tablespoons extra-virgin olive oil
2 tablespoons red wine vinegar

1/2 teaspoon granulated sugar
Salt, to taste
White pepper, to taste
Bibb lettuce, arugula, watercress
   or Boston lettuce
1 medium avocado, peeled and
   sliced thin (optional)

In a large, non-metallic container with a lid, combine mandarin orange segments, onion slices and poppy seeds.

In a bowl, combine olive oil, vinegar, sugar, salt and white pepper. Pour oil mixture over orange mixture. Toss to coat oranges and onions. Cover and refrigerate at least 2 hours.

Tear lettuce (choose one lettuce or a combination of several greens) into bite-size pieces; add to the mandarin orange mixture. Add avocado, if using. Toss well and serve immediately.

Marshmallow Delight

Lorrie Guttman
Food Editor, *Tallahassee Democrat*, Tallahassee, FL

Over the course of several summers, I have allowed my children, each in turn, to be judges of an annual recipe contest for children. It's a lot of fun to read the recipes and to watch my kids testing them. This fruit salad makes good use of marshmallows, an ingredient that seems to be a favorite with children. The recipe was sent in by an 8-year-old boy who listed cherries as an optional ingredient. With my family, maraschinos aren't optional in a fruit salad — they're a must!

Makes 4 servings

1 cup blackberries
   (or other berries), rinsed
   and drained
1 cup miniature marshmallows
1 cup diced pineapple
   (if using canned, drain liquid)

1 cup shredded coconut
1 cup dairy sour cream
1/2 cup maraschino cherries,
   drained

In a mixing bowl, combine blackberries, marshmallows, pineapple, coconut, sour cream and maraschino cherries. Refrigerate one hour.

Encourage teenagers to call home for a ride if they have been drinking.

Orange-Watercress Salad

Delia A. Hammock
Nutrition, Diet & Fitness Editor, *Good Housekeeping*, New York, NY

In my first attempt to land a position as assistant food editor at a magazine, I was asked to develop a recipe that included citrus fruit as an ingredient. This Orange-Watercress Salad was the result. I didn't get the job, but I've been enjoying the salad ever since.

Makes 4 servings

1 large bunch or 2 small bunches watercress

2 medium oranges, peeled, seeded, sectioned and sliced crosswise

1/3 cup sliced green onions (include some green tops)

1-1/2 tablespoons freshly squeezed lemon juice

1 tablespoon orange juice

1/4 teaspoon crushed dried mint

2 tablespoons olive oil or vegetable oil

1/4 teaspoon salt

Rinse watercress well. Remove and discard large stems. Dry leaves on paper towels; refrigerate.

When ready to serve, place watercress in a bowl or on a plate. Add orange sections and green onions.

In a small bowl, combine lemon juice, orange juice, mint, oil and salt; mix well. Pour dressing over salad. Toss gently but thoroughly. Serve immediately.

Peach Frost Salad

Clara Eschmann
Food Editor (Retired), *The Macon Telegraph and News*, Macon, GA

Because Georgia is "The Peach State," we use this luscious fruit as often as possible. This recipe was given to me by a close friend who is the wife of a peach farmer. It is easy to prepare and is a pretty accompaniment to any meal, especially on a hot summer day or evening. Many hostesses for bridal luncheons choose this delicacy as part of the menu because it is both popular and pretty.

Makes 8 servings

- 1 package (3 ounces) cream cheese, softened
- 1/2 cup heavy cream
- 1/4 cup mayonnaise
- 1 to 2 tablespoons lemon juice, depending on sweetness of peaches
- Dash salt
- 3 cups sliced fresh peaches (or one 30-ounce can sliced peaches, drained)
- 3/4 cup coarsely chopped pecans
- Lettuce leaves
- Dairy sour cream or mayonnaise, for garnish

In a mixing bowl, beat cream cheese and heavy cream until mixture is light and fluffy. Stir in mayonnaise, lemon juice and salt. Gently fold in peach slices and pecans. Pour into a 9x9x2-inch glass dish. Freeze several hours.

Remove from freezer 15 minutes before serving. Cut into squares; place each square in center of lettuce leaf on salad plate. Top each with a dollop of sour cream or mayonnaise.

Raspberry and Dried Cherry Salad

Ann Corell Wells
Food Editor, *The Grand Rapids Press*, Grand Rapids, MI

The red and green color combination makes this a pretty salad to serve during the Christmas holidays. It's the salad I always serve when my husband and I host our annual tree-trimming dinner. Dried cherries, available at gourmet and specialty stores, are a new way of using Michigan tart cherries. They give a piquant yet sweet flavor and extra texture to the salad. Be sure to serve this salad in a clear glass bowl to show off the colors.

Makes 12 servings

1 small head Bibb or
    Boston lettuce
1 head radicchio lettuce
1 head leaf lettuce or small
    head of Romaine lettuce
1/2 pound fresh spinach

1/2 to 3/4 cup sliced fresh
    mushrooms (optional)
1/4 cup thinly sliced green
    onions (optional)
1/3 cup toasted pecan pieces
1/4 cup dried tart cherries

Raspberry vinaigrette:
1 package (10 ounces) frozen
    unsweetened raspberries,
    thawed
1/4 cup raspberry vinegar

1/3 cup granulated sugar
3/4 cup vegetable oil
1/2 cup half-and-half or
    light cream

Rinse and drain Bibb lettuce, radicchio, leaf lettuce and spinach; tear into small pieces. Refrigerate, if desired, until ready to use.

For raspberry vinaigrette: Purée raspberries by pushing them through a fine sieve with the back of a wooden spoon. You should have at least 3/4 cup purée. In the container of an electric blender, combine vinegar and sugar. Blend until smooth. With blender running, slowly add oil, then slowly add half-and-half and raspberry purée. Mix well. Refrigerate until ready to serve. Shake well before serving.

To serve, combine chilled greens, mushrooms, green onions, pecans and dried cherries. Pour raspberry vinaigrette over salad; toss well.

Note: This salad is nice because everything can be prepared ahead of time and quickly assembled when ready to serve. To toast pecans, place nuts in a shallow baking pan; toast in a preheated 325-degree oven 5 to 10 minutes, stirring occasionally. Let cool.

Raspberry Yogurt and Fruit

Lori Longbotham
Free-Lance Food Writer, New York, NY

This fruit salad is great for breakfast, lunch or dinner. It also would be a great snack — mid-afternoon or midnight. It's good for you, and beautiful to look at. This is the perfect salad for a warm weather lunch on the deck, or to take on a picnic.

Makes 4 servings

1 package (10 ounces) frozen raspberries in light syrup, thawed
2 teaspoons cold water
1/2 teaspoon cornstarch
2 oranges, peeled, white pith removed, and sectioned
1 medium papaya, pared, seeded and cut into 1/2-inch cubes

1 medium banana, peeled and sliced
1/4 cup fresh blueberries, rinsed
10 fresh strawberries, rinsed, hulled and sliced
1 cup plain non-fat yogurt

Purée raspberries with syrup in food processor or blender. Strain; discard seeds. In a small saucepan over high heat, bring raspberry purée to boiling. In a small bowl, combine cold water and cornstarch; add to boiling purée. Cook over medium-high heat, whisking constantly, 2 to 4 minutes, or until slightly thickened. Transfer to mixing bowl. Put in freezer for 15 minutes, or until cold but not frozen.

In another bowl, combine orange sections, papaya, banana, blueberries and strawberries.

Whisk yogurt into chilled raspberry purée. Divide half the yogurt mixture among 4 bowls or goblets. Spoon fruit over yogurt mixture; top with remaining yogurt mixture.

Start saying "none for the road" instead of "one for the road."

Six-Cup Salad

Virginia Shufflebarger
Free-Lance Food Writer, Alexandria, VA

I like to prepare this salad when I don't have time to wash, peel and chop fresh fruit. It's quick and easy to put together and my family enjoys the combination of flavors. The recipe was given to me years ago by my sister-in-law, Barbara Shufflebarger, of Radford, Virginia. Variations of it have appeared in numerous church and club cookbooks. The salad is suitable for both winter and summer menus. I like to serve it in individual glass bowls.

Makes 6 servings

1 cup cottage cheese
1 cup dairy sour cream
1 cup fruit cocktail, well drained
1 cup pineapple chunks, well drained
1 cup miniature marshmallows

1 cup shredded coconut
Strawberries or sweet cherries, for garnish (optional)
Fresh mint leaves, for garnish (optional)

In a mixing bowl, combine cottage cheese and sour cream. Stir in fruit cocktail, pineapple, marshmallows and coconut. Mix well. Transfer to one large or six individual serving bowls. Garnish with strawberries or cherries and mint leaves, if desired.

Spiced Fresh Fruit Salad

Alice Handkins
Free-Lance Food Writer, Wichita, KS

Jicama and cinnamon give this salad a unique flavor and texture. When I prepare Mexican dishes, I always like to serve fruit to complement the hot spiciness of the other foods. This is a salad I developed especially for this purpose, although it works well with many other types of food as well. Guests who are not familiar with jicama always comment on the delightful crunchiness it gives to this salad. They often think it is coconut.

Makes 8 to 10 servings

1 cup peeled, diced jicama
2 oranges, peeled and cut into
   1/2-inch pieces
2 cups fresh pineapple chunks
   (1/2-inch chunks)

1/2 cup orange juice
1/4 cup confectioners' sugar
1/4 teaspoon ground cinnamon
2 bananas

In a mixing bowl, combine jicama, oranges, pineapple, orange juice, confectioners' sugar and cinnamon. Refrigerate one hour, stirring occasionally.

When ready to serve, peel bananas and slice them into the salad; stir gently to mix. Serve at once.

   Please say "Yes" the next time a MADD volunteer asks for your support.

Spiced Pear Salad

Toni Burks
Food Editor, *Roanoke Times & World-News*, Roanoke, VA

One of my mother's favorite salads for an extra-special family dinner consisted of a canned pear half stuffed with a mixture of cream cheese and chopped pecans and centered on a crisp lettuce leaf. It was good — and still is — and is easy to assemble. This is kind of the same idea, although it takes more time to prepare. Just between friends, it's a lot more special and it is better than just good.

Makes 8 servings

1/2 cup firmly packed
   brown sugar
1/2 cup orange juice
1 tablespoon balsamic vinegar
1/4 teaspoon ground cinnamon
1/4 teaspoon ground nutmeg
Dash ground cloves

4 ripe but firm Bartlett pears,
   cored and halved lengthwise
   (peel only if desired)
1 package (8 ounces) cream
   cheese
1/4 to 1/3 cup finely chopped
   pecans
Bibb or Boston lettuce leaves

In a 10-inch skillet or wide saucepan, combine brown sugar, orange juice, vinegar, cinnamon, nutmeg and cloves. Bring to a boil. Reduce heat. Add pear halves. Cover and simmer 5 to 6 minutes, or until pears are tender. Remove from heat. Transfer pears carefully to storage dish and pour poaching liquid over them. Cover and refrigerate until thoroughly chilled.

Just before serving, cut cream cheese into 8 pieces. Shape each piece into a ball, then roll balls in chopped pecans to coat.

To assemble salad, line 8 salad plates with lettuce; place a pear half on each. Spoon poaching liquid over pears. Place a cheese ball in center of each pear.

Strawberry-Spinach Salad

Leona Carlson
Food Writer (Retired), *Rockford Register Star*, Rockford, IL

A strawberry-spinach salad was on the menu at a luncheon I attended some years ago, and it was love at first taste. Unfortunately, the recipe was not available. I searched unsuccessfully for years until my daughter-in-law in California gave me a cookbook containing a similar recipe. I made a few changes and have served the resulting salad many times, always to rave reviews. Tossed in a large, clear glass bowl, it looks beautiful.

Makes 10 servings

2 bunches fresh spinach
1 quart fresh strawberries
1/2 teaspoon minced onion
1/4 cup cider vinegar
1/4 cup vegetable oil
1/4 cup honey

1/4 teaspoon Worcestershire
sauce
2 tablespoons toasted sesame
seeds
1 teaspoon poppy seeds

Rinse spinach leaves thoroughly; tear into bite-size pieces. Drain on paper towels.

Hull and rinse strawberries. Cut in half or leave whole, depending on size. Drain on paper towels.

In container of electric blender, combine onion, vinegar, oil, honey and Worcestershire sauce; blend until smooth. Stir in sesame seeds and poppy seeds.

In a large salad bowl, combine spinach and strawberries. Toss with dressing. Serve immediately.

Note: I rarely add all the dressing because I dislike soggy salads. But not to worry; the dressing keeps well in the refrigerator. The salad, alas, wilts after a few hours in the refrigerator.

Stuffed Fig Salad

Barbara Burklo
Food Editor (Retired), *Santa Cruz Sentinel*, Santa Cruz, CA

About 97 percent of the nation's fig crop is grown in the Fresno, California, area. Frank Domenik, who was president of the Valley Fig Growers before he retired in Santa Cruz, gave me this salad recipe along with other fig recipes I used in a food section story.

Makes 4 servings

1 head Bibb or Boston lettuce, rinsed, drained and torn into bite-size pieces	1 cup chopped walnuts
1 bunch watercress, rinsed, drained and cut into sprigs	16 Calimyrna or Mission dried figs
1/2 cup sliced green onions	16 small chunks Gorgonzola cheese
	1/2 cup balsamic vinegar

Toss together lettuce, watercress, green onions and walnuts. Divide among 4 salad plates; refrigerate.

Cut stems off figs. Using a small knife, carefully rotate tip of knife to make an opening in the stem of each fig. Form a pocket in the opening with forefinger. Stuff a small chunk of cheese into pocket of each fig. Place cheese-stuffed figs in a baking dish. Bake in a preheated 350-degree oven 10 minutes, or until cheese starts to melt.

Arrange hot figs on greens on salad plates, allowing 4 figs per serving. Drizzle balsamic vinegar over salads.

Waldorf Renovation

Narcisse S. Cadgène
Free-Lance Writer, New York, NY

Even a grand old lady like the Waldorf Salad can use a facelift every so often. This adaptation travels well for lunch at the office or school.

Makes 4 appetizer servings or 8 salad-course servings

Spiced Pecans:

1 cup pecan halves	1/4 teaspoon granulated garlic
Water	1/8 to 1/4 teaspoon salt
2 teaspoons butter	1/8 teaspoon black pepper
2 teaspoons Worcestershire sauce	1/8 teaspoon cayenne pepper
4 teaspoons granulated sugar	

Salad:

1 very large or 2 small apples (preferably sweet)	3/4 cup mayonnaise
1 tablespoon lemon juice	3 ounces semi-dry or hard goat cheese crumbled into
1 cup diced celery	1/2- inch pieces (optional)
1/2 cup stemmed seedless grapes	

Salad Bed (optional):

8 cups salad greens, rinsed and well drained	1/4 cup vegetable oil
2 tablespoons red wine vinegar	Salt, to taste
	Black pepper, to taste

For the spiced pecans: Place pecan halves in a skillet or wok (preferably one with a non-stick surface). Barely cover pecans with water. Bring to a simmer over high heat; drain immediately. To drained pecans in skillet, add butter, Worcestershire sauce, sugar, garlic, salt, pepper and cayenne; mix well. Cook over medium-to-high heat, stirring constantly, until mixture caramelizes. Spread pecans on a plate to cool.

For the salad: Rinse, halve, and core apple(s). Dice apple(s) into pieces about the size of grapes. Mix apple pieces with lemon juice to prevent discoloration. Add celery, grapes and Spiced Pecans to apples; mix. Stir in mayonnaise; mix well. Add cheese, if using.

For the salad bed: At serving time, toss greens with vinegar, oil, salt and pepper. Arrange greens on individual plates. Top with a scoop of apple mixture. Serve immediately.

Volunteer to be a Designated Driver when you go out with a group.

MOLDED
SALADS

Apricot-Cream Salad

Carolyn Flournoy
Food Columnist, *The Times*, Shreveport, LA

If you are looking for a salad that appeals to both men and women, young and old, sophisticated and plain tastes; that is easy to prepare and serve; that can be made ahead and is easy on the purse — here it is! This saucy apricot mold looks (and is) so simple, yet I reap many compliments every time I serve it. If you adore apricots, this is Nirvana.

Makes 6 to 8 servings

1 pound pitted, dried apricots	15 large marshmallows, diced
2 cups water	2 cups dairy sour cream
1 package (6 ounces)	2 teaspoons lemon juice
orange-flavored gelatin	Lettuce leaves

Combine apricots and 2 cups water in a saucepan; bring to a boil. Reduce heat and simmer 12 minutes, or until apricots are soft. Drain apricots, reserving cooking liquid.

Prepare gelatin according to package directions, substituting reserved apricot cooking liquid for part of the water. Refrigerate until partly thickened.

Meanwhile, mash apricots or purée apricots in a food processor or blender. Add mashed apricots to partly thickened gelatin. Pour mixture into a lightly oiled 1-1/2-quart mold. Refrigerate until firm.

In a bowl, combine marshmallows, sour cream and lemon juice. Refrigerate, covered, overnight.

To serve salad, unmold gelatin onto a platter lined with lettuce leaves. Serve marshmallow mixture as a dressing for the gelatin salad.

Select a Designated Driver when your outing will involve alcohol.

Asheville Salad

Carole Currie
Lifestyle Editor, *Asheville Citizen*, Asheville, NC

In the days when Asheville's Battery Park Hotel was one of the country's leading summer resorts, one of the recipes that originated from chefs at the hotel was Asheville Salad, a rich, tomato-based, congealed salad. Apparently the hotel chef was generous in sharing his recipe with visitors, because hostesses in Asheville often served the salad in their homes and still do. The recipe has been passed down through families. Whenever the recipe is requested in recipe-swap columns, it never fails to draw responses. The original recipe called for an 8-ounce package of cream cheese, a cup of mayonnaise and three chopped hard-cooked eggs, but the result is a rather bland salad. I modified the recipe, adding celery, onion and green pepper to give the salad a little zip.

Makes 8 to 10 servings

1 can (10-1/2 ounces) condensed cream of tomato soup, undiluted
1 soup can water
1 package (3 ounces) cream cheese, cut into cubes
2 envelopes unflavored gelatin
1/2 cup minus 2 tablespoons cold water
2 tablespoons lemon juice
Dash Worcestershire sauce
1/4 cup light mayonnaise
1 cup chopped celery
2 tablespoons finely chopped onion
1/4 cup chopped green bell pepper
1/4 cup chopped pimento-stuffed green olives
Salt and black pepper, to taste
Salad greens or watercress, for garnish

In a saucepan, combine tomato soup and soup can of water; bring to a simmer. Add cream cheese and simmer gently, stirring constantly, until cheese is softened. Beat with wire whisk until mixture is thoroughly blended.

Soften gelatin in cold water; add to hot soup mixture and stir until dissolved. Let cool. Add lemon juice, Worcestershire sauce and mayonnaise; mix well. Refrigerate until mixture is the consistency of egg whites. Gently stir in celery, onion, green pepper and olives. Season to taste with salt and pepper. Pour into a lightly oiled 1-1/2-quart mold. Refrigerate until firm. Unmold on a bed of salad greens or watercress.

Blueberry Salad

Clara Eschmann
Food Editor (retired), *The Macon Telegraph and News*, Macon, GA

This salad is an easy one that uses ingredients that are available year-round. The idea is one that I helped develop for a frozen food company promotion. It was well received by the company and also has been popular when served to guests in my home. It's pretty as well as tasty.

Makes 12 servings

1 can (15 ounces) crushed
    pineapple
2 packages (3 ounces each)
    lemon-flavored gelatin
1 cup boiling water
1 can (6 ounces) pineapple juice
2 cups frozen blueberries,
    thawed and drained
    (or equivalent fresh berries)

1 package (8 ounces) cream
    cheese, softened
1/4 cup granulated sugar
1 cup dairy sour cream
1 teaspoon vanilla
1/2 cup chopped pecans

Drain crushed pineapple, reserving juice. In a medium mixing bowl, combine gelatin and boiling water; stir to completely dissolve gelatin. Add reserved juice from crushed pineapple and the pineapple juice. Refrigerate 45 minutes, or until gelatin is soft-set, stirring once. Stir in drained pineapple and blueberries. Spoon into a 13x9x2-inch dish. Refrigerate 30 to 45 minutes, or until firm.

In a medium mixing bowl with an electric mixer on high speed, beat cream cheese and sugar until light and fluffy. Add sour cream and vanilla; mix well. Spread evenly over blueberry gelatin layer. Sprinkle pecans over top. Refrigerate 1 to 2 hours. To serve, cut into squares.

Buttermilk Salad

Stacy Lam
Reporter, *The Macon Telegraph*, Macon, GA

Recipes don't get any easier than this gelatin salad — four ingredients mixed in one saucepan. It's a light, summertime salad. The buttermilk gives the salad a cottage cheese texture with just a hint of tartness. To vary this salad, add fruits or nuts with the whipped topping.

Never let friends or relatives drink and drive.

Makes 8 servings

1 can (8 ounces) crushed
    pineapple
1 package (6 ounces) orange-
    or apricot-flavored gelatin

2 cups buttermilk
1 container (9-3/4 ounces)
    frozen non-dairy whipped
    topping, thawed

In a medium saucepan, bring pineapple with its juice to a boil. Remove from heat. Stir in gelatin until well dissolved. Add buttermilk. Refrigerate 45 minutes, or until partly set. Fold in whipped topping, blending well. Pour into 8 serving dishes. Refrigerate until firm.

Charger Inn Cranberry Salad

Sally Cappon
Food Columnist, *Santa Barbara News-Press*, Santa Barbara, CA

Under the enthusiastic tutelage of instructor Ginny Folan, students in the Regional Occupational Program at Dos Pueblos High School in Santa Barbara run the school's popular Charger Inn. While learning techniques of food preparation and restaurant management, students provide delicious snacks and lunches for the school's staff and visitors. This cranberry salad is an attractive and tasty addition to the Charger Inn Thanksgiving dinner.

Makes 12 servings

1 package (6 ounces)
    raspberry-flavored gelatin
1-1/2 cups boiling water
12 ice cubes
1/2 pound fresh or frozen
    cranberries, ground

1 can (8 ounces) crushed
    pineapple, drained
1/2 cup chopped walnuts
1/2 cup chopped celery
Salad greens
Whipped cream

In a large bowl, combine gelatin and boiling water; stir to dissolve. Add ice cubes; stir until melted. Refrigerate 10 minutes, or until slightly set. Add ground cranberries, pineapple, walnuts and celery. Pour into a 13x9x2-inch pan. Refrigerate until firm.

To serve, cut into squares and serve on salad greens. Garnish each serving with a dollop of whipped cream.

Corned Beef Salad

Barbara Burklo
Food Editor (Retired), *Santa Cruz Sentinel*, Santa Cruz, CA

This hearty, flavorful salad is a nice combination of meat protein and crisp vegetables. My friend Winnie Urbschat of Columbiana, Ohio, shared it with me. It's a perfect — and much praised — luncheon dish.

Makes 4 servings

1 package (3 ounces)
  lemon-flavored gelatin
1 cup boiling water
3/4 to 1 cup mayonnaise
1 can (12 ounces) corned beef,
  shredded

1 cup chopped celery
1/2 green bell pepper, chopped
3 hard-cooked eggs, peeled
  and chopped
Lettuce

Combine gelatin and boiling water in a large bowl; stir until gelatin is dissolved. Let mixture come to room temperature. Add 3/4 cup mayonnaise and mix well. Fold in corned beef, celery, green pepper and eggs. Mix well. If needed, add remaining 1/4 cup mayonnaise. Turn into a lightly oiled 13x9x2-inch dish or 1-quart ring mold. Refrigerate until set. Serve on lettuce-lined salad plates.

Famous Lime Salad

Louise Dodd
Food Editor, *Courier Herald*, Dublin, GA

When I moved to a small mid-Georgia town years ago to help my new husband establish himself as a country doctor, one lady in the town, Lizzie Lee, literally took us under her wing as two of her children. With my feet firmly planted under her table hundreds of times, I enjoyed some truly magnificent, yet plain, Southern cooking. This salad is one of her specialties and one that later became my children's favorite recipe. I never serve a special occasion family meal without it.

Makes 10 servings

1 package (3 ounces)
   lime-flavored gelatin
1 cup miniature marshmallows
1 package (3 ounces) cream
   cheese, softened
2 cups boiling water

1 cup heavy cream
1/2 cup mayonnaise
1 can (5-1/4 ounces) crushed
   pineapple, drained
1/2 cup chopped pecans
   (optional)

In a large mixing bowl, combine gelatin, marshmallows and cream cheese. Add boiling water; stir until mixture is creamy, making sure gelatin is dissolved. Let the mixture cool in the refrigerator until it begins to gel.

In a large mixing bowl with an electric mixer or hand beater, whip cream until stiff peaks form. Fold in mayonnaise and pineapple.

Remove gelatin mixture from the refrigerator. Beat it until it becomes light in color and texture. Fold in whipped cream mixture. Pour into a lightly oiled Bundt pan or 10 individual salad molds. Refrigerate until set.

Florida Grapefruit Salad

Caroline Stuart
Contributing Editor, *Hudson Valley Magazine*, Poughkeepsie, NY

This old-fashioned grapefruit salad is a favorite among Floridians. It is perfect as an accompaniment to a meal on a hot summer day. When preparing this salad you can choose any kind of grapefruit, but the ideal fruit is a fresh, pink variety which adds a delightful blush color. You can prepare this salad up to two days prior to serving; tightly cover salad and store in the refrigerator.

Makes 16 servings

Approximately 4 medium-size pink grapefruit
Juice of 1/2 lemon
3/4 cup granulated sugar
3 envelopes unflavored gelatin
1/2 cup cold water

1 cup boiling water
1-1/2 packages (8 ounces each) cream cheese, softened
1/2 cup finely chopped pecans
1/4 teaspoon grated lemon peel

Peel grapefruit, completely removing the white pith and membrane; reserve the grapefruit sections. By hand, squeeze any remaining juice from the grapefruit pulp and add to the grapefruit sections. Remove and discard any seeds. You should have 4 cups grapefruit sections with juice.

Place grapefruit sections and juice, lemon juice and sugar in a large mixing bowl.

Combine gelatin and cold water in a small bowl. Add boiling water; stir until gelatin is dissolved. Add gelatin mixture to grapefruit mixture.

In a small bowl, combine cream cheese, pecans and lemon peel. To make mixture spreadable, add 2/3 cup liquid from the grapefruit mixture; cream well with a hand mixer.

Pour half of the grapefruit mixture into a 13x9x2-inch pan, distributing grapefruit sections evenly. Refrigerate 30 minutes, until partly set.

Spread cream cheese mixture over partly set gelatin, making a smooth, even layer. Pour remaining grapefruit mixture over cream cheese layer, being careful not to disturb cream cheese. Refrigerate several hours, or until firmly set.

Cut into 3x2-inch pieces. Serve on the dinner plate along with the meal or serve as a side salad on a bed of lettuce.

July Salad

Virginia Shufflebarger
Free-Lance Food Writer, Alexandria, VA

In July, the tables at the Mount Vernon Farmers' Market are piled high with fragrant, rosy peaches. Shoppers line up to buy fat, dusky blueberries. At this market, all the produce has been grown locally so the fruit is orchard-fresh and juicy. I shop there for the ingredients to make this salad which is not only pretty, but also delicious.

Makes 6 servings

1 package (3 ounces) peach-flavored gelatin	1/4 cup diced honeydew melon
1 cup boiling water	1/2 cup blueberries, rinsed and drained
3/4 cup cold water	1/4 cup sliced seedless grapes
1 cup sliced ripe peaches	Lettuce or other salad greens

Completely dissolve gelatin in boiling water. Thoroughly mix in cold water. Refrigerate until mixture begins to thicken. Blend in peaches, honeydew, blueberries and grapes, distributing fruit throughout gelatin mixture. Refrigerate several hours, or overnight, until firm. Serve on lettuce or other greens.

Layered Cranberry Salad

Louise Dodd
Food Editor, *Courier Herald*, Dublin, GA

The first time I staged a cooking contest for the newspaper, the plans were ambitious. Not only did we give the winner a cash award, but we also transported her and her guests in a chauffeur-driven limousine to my home for a seven-course candlelight and wine dinner served by the newsroom staff, including the editor. The winning recipe that warranted this grand occasion? This scrumptious-tasting salad that the winner said came from a cookbook so old and yellow that the pages were falling out. That doesn't diminish its timeliness for today's appetites. It's truly a great recipe.

Makes 25 servings

Cranberry Layer:

1 envelope unflavored gelatin
1/4 cup cold water
1 can (16 ounces) whole-berry
   cranberry sauce

1 can (9 ounces) crushed
   pineapple, drained
1/2 cup chopped walnuts
1 tablespoon lemon juice

Chicken Layer:

1 envelope unflavored gelatin
3/4 cup cold water, divided
1 cup mayonnaise
3 tablespoons lemon juice
3/4 teaspoon salt

2 cups cooked, diced chicken
1/2 cup finely chopped celery
2 tablespoons finely chopped
   fresh parsley

For cranberry layer: Combine gelatin and cold water in the top of a double boiler; over hot water, heat and stir until gelatin dissolves. Add cranberry sauce, pineapple, walnuts and lemon juice. Mix well. Pour mixture into lightly oiled 3-quart baking dish. Refrigerate until firm.

For chicken layer: Combine gelatin and 1/4 cup cold water in the top of a double boiler; over hot water, heat and stir until gelatin dissolves. Blend in mayonnaise, remaining 1/2 cup cold water, lemon juice and salt. Add the chicken, celery and parsley. Stir to mix.

Pour chicken mixture over the firm cranberry layer. Refrigerate until firm. To serve, cut into squares.

Learn more about MADD's Speakers Bureau.

Melt-In-Your-Mouth Molded Mushroom Salad

Laura Barton
Free-Lance Food Writer, Portland, OR

As a child, I would pick mushrooms out of a salad and leave them on my plate, but as I grew older, I began to love mushrooms. This salad certainly attests to my change of tastebuds. It was served at a summertime potluck party where I worked as a lifeguard and swim instructor during college. The mother of one of my young swimming students brought it. I taught her son to swim, and she gave me her recipe — a fair trade!

Makes 6 servings

2 envelopes unflavored gelatin
1/2 cup water
1 package (8 ounces) cream cheese, cut into cubes
1 can (10-1/2 ounces) condensed cream of mushroom soup, undiluted
1 pound fresh mushrooms, sliced
2 tablespoons butter

1 cup diced celery
1 cup finely diced onions
1 cup mayonnaise
1 can (4 ounces) sliced black olives, drained
1 tablespoon prepared horseradish
1 tablespoon white pepper
1 tablespoon garlic powder

Soften the gelatin in water. In a medium saucepan over low heat, combine gelatin mixture, cream cheese and soup; blend until smooth. Let cool.

In a large skillet, sauté mushrooms in butter until lightly browned. Add to cream cheese mixture. Add celery, onions, mayonnaise, olives, horseradish, white pepper and garlic powder. Mix well. Pour mixture into a lightly oiled 2-quart mold. Refrigerate until firm.

Molded Cucumber Salad

June Ann Gladfelter
Managing Editor/Features, *The Express*, Easton, PA

Even people who do not like cucumbers like this salad. The first bite sometimes isn't so good, but the taste is addictive; you keep going back to it. This recipe makes a pretty molded salad that's perfect for special occasions. For variation, use zucchini instead of cucumber.

Makes 8 servings

1 package (3 ounces)
   lime-flavored gelatin
1 cup boiling water
1 medium cucumber, finely
   chopped
1 medium onion, finely chopped
1-1/2 cups cream-style
   cottage cheese

1 teaspoon white vinegar
1/2 cup salad dressing or
   mayonnaise
1/2 cup chopped walnuts or
   pecans
Lettuce leaves

In a medium bowl, dissolve gelatin in boiling water. Set aside to cool.

In another bowl, combine cucumber, onion and cottage cheese. (Or, if desired, purée cucumber, onion and cottage cheese in a blender.)

In a large bowl, combine cucumber mixture, vinegar and mayonnaise-type salad dressing. Stir in gelatin mixture and walnuts; mix well.

Pour into a lightly oiled 4-cup mold. Refrigerate until firm. To serve, unmold onto crisp lettuce leaves.

MADD needs your help to stop drinking and driving.

Molded Fish Salad

Ann Hattes
Free-Lance Food and Travel Writer, Hartland, WI

My aunt enjoyed cooking and had an extensive collection of cookbooks. In fact, she enjoyed cookbooks as pleasure reading and could tell what a recipe would taste like just from reading its ingredients. On my birthdays, I often would find a hand-copied recipe from her extensive collection enclosed in the greeting card. This is one of them.

My husband doesn't care for gelatin, but he does like this recipe. When prepared with lobster or salmon, it makes a good salad to serve to guests as well as to family.

Makes 4 to 6 servings

1 can (10-1/2 ounces) condensed cream of tomato soup, undiluted
3 packages (8 ounces each) cream cheese, softened
2 envelopes unflavored gelatin
1/2 cup cold water
1 cup diced celery
2 teaspoons minced onion
1 can (16 ounces) tuna, lobster or salmon, well drained
1 cup salad dressing or mayonnaise

In a large saucepan, combine soup and cream cheese. Cook over low heat, stirring constantly, until mixture is smooth and hot.

Soften gelatin in cold water; let stand for about 3 minutes. Add gelatin mixture to hot soup mixture. Remove from heat and let mixture cool. Add celery, onion and fish. Let stand about 20 minutes, then fold in mayonnaise-type salad dressing.

Pour into a lightly oiled 1-quart mold. Refrigerate overnight to let flavors blend.

Molded Gazpacho Salad

Alice Handkins
Free-Lance Food Writer, Wichita, KS

Gazpacho is a favorite soup of many people. It takes on a slightly different form, though, in this salad with its wonderful sour cream dressing. Sometimes I like to serve this for a light summer luncheon, with a bowl of tortilla chips and a plate of freshly sliced avocados, celery strips and olives.

Makes 8 to 10 servings

3 cups tomato juice
2 envelopes unflavored gelatin
2 tablespoons cider vinegar
2 tablespoons lemon juice
1/4 teaspoon garlic powder
1-1/2 teaspoons salt
1/4 teaspoon black pepper
1/4 teaspoon hot pepper sauce
3 tomatoes, peeled and
   diced (about 2-1/2 cups)

1 cup finely chopped cucumber
1/2 cup finely chopped green
   bell pepper
1/4 cup finely chopped onion
1/4 cup finely chopped celery
2/3 cup dairy sour cream
2/3 cup mayonnaise

Pour tomato juice into a saucepan; stir in gelatin. Let stand 2 minutes. Bring tomato juice to a simmer over medium-low heat. Stir until gelatin is dissolved. Add vinegar, lemon juice, garlic powder, salt, black pepper and hot pepper sauce; mix well. Refrigerate until mixture begins to thicken slightly.

Add tomatoes, cucumber, green pepper, onion and celery to tomato juice mixture. Pour into a lightly oiled 1-1/2-quart ring mold. Refrigerate until firm.

Meanwhile, combine sour cream and mayonnaise; refrigerate until time to serve salad. Unmold salad onto a plate. Serve sour cream dressing in center of salad ring.

Orange-Avocado Salad

Constance Hay
Free-Lance Food Writer, Columbia, MD

Summer is the perfect time to make this salad — when it's too hot to cook and people want something cool and light to eat. Serve it for a refreshing lunch or supper, accompanied by a loaf of crusty bread and a pitcher of iced tea.

Makes 4 servings

1 package (3 ounces)
    lemon-flavored gelatin
1 cup boiling water
1 cup cold water

2 oranges, peeled and
    cut into segments
1 avocado, peeled and diced

Dressing:

2/3 cup mayonnaise
1/3 cup dairy sour cream
2 tablespoons chili sauce
1 can (5 ounces) tiny shrimp,
    drained

2 hard-cooked eggs, peeled
    and chopped
3 green onions, finely sliced
Lettuce leaves

In a large mixing bowl, dissolve gelatin in boiling water. Add cold water; refrigerate until thickened, but not set. Gently fold in oranges and avocado. Pour into a 9x5x3-inch pan. Refrigerate until set.

For dressing: Combine mayonnaise, sour cream and chili sauce. Fold in shrimp, eggs and green onions.

Cut gelatin into four portions; place each on a lettuce-lined plate. Top each portion with dressing or pass dressing separately.

Orange-Pineapple Salad

Susan Ruddiman
Food Editor, *The Mississippi Press*, Pascagoula, MS

Here on the Mississippi Gulf Coast, where the summer seems to be six months long, this salad is popular with my family because it is so cool to eat. My Uncle Edsel serves this salad quite often in the summer when the family gathers for dinner at noon on Sundays (we simply call it Noon Dinner, a tradition started by my grandmother). Although gelatin is used in this salad, it's not prepared in the usual manner. We usually serve this salad on a simple bed of lettuce.

Makes 9 servings

1 can (16 ounces) crushed pineapple, well drained

2 cans (11 ounces each) mandarin oranges, well drained

1 container (8 ounces) frozen non-dairy whipped topping, thawed

1 carton (8 ounces) cottage cheese

1 package (3 ounces) orange-flavored gelatin

In a large mixing bowl, combine pineapple, mandarin oranges, whipped topping, cottage cheese and dry gelatin. Mix well with a spoon or spatula. Pour into a 9x9x2-inch glass dish. Refrigerate overnight. Cut into squares to serve.

Be a responsible host.

Pineapple Pepper Salad

Florence Roggenbach
Living/Food Editor, *Norfolk Daily News*, Norfolk, NE

When I was a small girl, spending vacation time with Grandma and Grandpa was a special treat. One reason was that mealtime was a big deal for Grandma. She could even serve foods I didn't like — and they tasted good! Grandma rented rooms, so there usually were at least two renters at each meal. That might be one reason Grandma made a special effort to serve fancy meals every day of the week.

Makes 6 servings

6 small green bell peppers	2 tablespoons finely chopped
1 envelope unflavored gelatin	pimento
2 tablespoons pineapple juice	Salt
3/4 cup crushed pineapple	Paprika
1 package (3 ounces) cream	Lettuce
cheese, softened	Mayonnaise
2 tablespoons chopped walnuts	

Rinse green peppers in cold water. Cut a slice from the top of each. Remove and discard seeds and membranes. Set peppers aside.

In the top of a small double boiler over boiling water, soften gelatin in pineapple juice; stir until dissolved.

In a mixing bowl, combine gelatin mixture, pineapple, cream cheese, walnuts and pimento. Season to taste with salt and paprika.

Fill peppers with equal portions of gelatin mixture. Refrigerate until gelatin mixture is firm.

To serve, cut filled peppers into rings; arrange rings on lettuce. Top each serving with a dollop of mayonnaise.

Prune Aspic

Doris Reynolds
Food Columnist, *Naples Daily News*, Naples, FL

There's no doubt about it, prunes are the Rodney Dangerfield of fruits. In spite of the fact that they are loaded with fiber, minerals, vitamins and good taste, prunes are ridiculed and get little or no respect here in the United States. Europeans, however, are much more appreciative of prunes and consider them a delicacy. This dish was served at a church supper. The woman who brought it was kind enough to give me the recipe. It is particularly delicious served with roast pork or pork chops.

Makes 12 servings

2 envelopes unflavored gelatin
1/2 cup cold water
3-1/2 cups bottled prune juice
4 cups cooked prunes
2 tablespoons lemon juice

1 package (8 ounces) cream
    cheese, softened
2 to 3 tablespoons milk
Orange slices

Soften gelatin in cold water. In a large saucepan, heat prune juice. Add gelatin mixture; stir until dissolved. Remove from heat. Refrigerate until mixture is partly set.

Pit and coarsely chop the cooked prunes. Add prunes and lemon juice to partly set gelatin mixture. Pour into a lightly oiled 1-1/2-quart ring mold. Refrigerate until set.

In a small bowl, combine cream cheese and milk; mix until cream cheese is smooth.

Turn prune aspic out onto a serving plate; garnish with orange slices. Fill center of ring mold with cream cheese mixture.

Stop serving drinks at least 90 minutes before the party ends.

Raspberry Walnut Thanksgiving Salad

Barbara Yost
Feature Writer, *The Phoenix Gazette*, Phoenix, AZ

Every year I share Thanksgiving dinner with my friend Mary Ann Nock and her family. I created this salad as my contribution to the feast, and now it's become as much a tradition as her mother's pumpkin pies. Mary Ann's husband, Jack, doesn't like nuts, so I always leave the nuts out of one portion and mark it especially for him. He's thankful for that.

Makes 6 servings

1 package (3 ounces) raspberry-flavored gelatin
1 cup boiling water
1 cup cold water
1 package (8 ounces) cream cheese, softened

1 package (10 ounces) frozen raspberries, thawed and well drained
1/2 cup chopped walnuts
Lettuce leaves

In a medium mixing bowl, combine gelatin and boiling water; stir until gelatin is dissolved. Add cold water; mix well.

In another bowl, combine half of the gelatin mixture with the cream cheese; blend well. Pour mixture into bottom of a lightly oiled 3-cup mold. Refrigerate until mixture is almost set.

Add raspberries and walnuts to remaining half of gelatin mixture. Leave at room temperature until cream cheese mixture is almost set. Pour raspberry mixture over cream cheese mixture. Refrigerate until firm. To serve, turn onto plate covered with lettuce leaves.

Strawberry Pretzel Salad

Toni Burks
Food Editor, *Roanoke Times & World-News*, Roanoke, VA

At potlucks, church suppers, family reunions and any other occasion where a bunch of people come together to share good times and good food, everyone oohs and aahs over the gelatin salads. Not savory aspics that are really salads; rather, sweet fruit mixtures that are really desserts. Everyone enjoys them last while they ask for the recipe. A co-worker, who got this recipe at a church supper, entered it in an inner-office cooking contest and won second place — in the dessert category.

Makes 12 servings

2 cups coarsely crushed pretzels
3/4 cup margarine, melted
1 cup plus 3 tablespoons granulated sugar, divided
1 package (8 ounces) cream cheese, softened
1 container (8 ounces) frozen non-dairy whipped topping, thawed

1 package (6 ounces) strawberry-flavored gelatin
1 cup boiling water
1/2 cup miniature marshmallows
2 packages (10 ounces each) frozen sliced strawberries, thawed

Combine crushed pretzels, margarine and 3 tablespoons sugar; mix well. Press into a 13x9x2-inch baking dish. Bake in a preheated 400-degree oven 8 minutes. Remove from oven and let cool completely.

In a large mixing bowl with an electric mixer, beat cream cheese and remaining 1 cup sugar until well blended. Fold in whipped topping. Spread over cooled pretzel crust. Refrigerate until chilled.

In a mixing bowl, dissolve gelatin in boiling water. Add marshmallows and stir until melted. Add strawberries with their juice. Let stand 10 minutes. Pour over cream cheese layer. Refrigerate until firm. Cut into squares to serve.

Friends keep friends alive. Don't let your friends drink and drive.

Sweet-and-Sour Beet Salad

Louise Dodd
Food Editor, *Courier Herald*, Dublin, GA

This tangy, sweet salad is one I jotted down on the back of a bridge score sheet. All the other players at bridge club that day have a copy just like it at home because everybody had to have the recipe. This versatile recipe is colorful and goes well with so many meats, especially beef, because of the horseradish flavor. It's a grand-slam winner anytime.

Makes 6 to 8 servings

1 can (5-1/4 ounces) crushed pineapple
1 package (3 ounces) lemon-flavored gelatin
1 can (16 ounces) julienned beets, drained
2 teaspoons grated onion
1 tablespoon white vinegar

1 tablespoon prepared horseradish
1/2 teaspoon salt
1 teaspoon granulated sugar
1 cup finely chopped celery
Dairy sour cream, mayonnaise and sliced pimento, stuffed olives, for garnish (optional)

Drain pineapple, reserving pineapple liquid. Set pineapple aside. Add enough water to reserved pineapple liquid to make 1-3/4 cups liquid.

In a small saucepan, bring liquid to a boil. Remove from heat. Add gelatin and stir until gelatin is dissolved. Refrigerate until mixture is the consistency of egg whites.

In a large mixing bowl, combine gelatin mixture, reserved pineapple, beets, onion, vinegar, horseradish, salt, sugar and celery. Pour into 6 individual molds or one lightly oiled 6-cup mold. Refrigerate until salad is completely set.

Garnish each serving with a dollop of sour cream or margaine and a slice of olive.

Tomato Aspic

Leona Carlson
Food Writer (Retired), *Rockford Register Star*, Rockford, IL

> *This is the perfect salad for cholesterol-counters, and it's so tasty and colorful. This recipe has more character than any other aspic I have found in years of exploring cookbooks coast to coast. Its spicy flavor and bright red hue perk up any meal, especially a luncheon quiche or a brunch egg casserole.*

Makes 6 to 8 servings

3 cups tomato juice
1/2 teaspoon granulated sugar
1/2 teaspoon ground cloves
1 tablespoon minced onion
1 tablespoon Italian seasoning

2 envelopes unflavored gelatin
1/2 cup water
1 teaspoon lemon juice
2 teaspoons Worcestershire sauce

In a large saucepan, combine tomato juice, sugar, cloves, onion and Italian seasoning. Simmer over medium heat 15 minutes. Remove from heat.

In a small container, soak gelatin in water until softened. Add to hot tomato juice mixture. Stir until gelatin dissolves. Add lemon juice and Worcestershire sauce; mix well.

Pour into a lightly oiled 8-inch square pan or 1-quart ring mold. Refrigerate until set.

Note: If desired, center of ring mold can be filled with 1 cup cooked tiny shrimp mixed with mayonnaise and chopped fresh chives.

Take responsibility for your actions about drinking and driving.

PASTA, POTATO &RICE SALADS

Ballard Adobe Rice Salad

Sally Cappon
Food Columnist, *Santa Barbara News-Press*, Santa Barbara, CA

The old Ballard adobe served as a 19th-century stagecoach stop on Alamo Pintado Road in the Santa Ynez Valley northwest of Santa Barbara. Dale Rossi's family has restored the thick-walled adobe to a charming family home. Dale, an accomplished artist whose paintings of the ranching countryside grace the adobe walls, served this salad for a meeting in her home of the Santa Barbara Historical Society docents. She shared the recipe with me for a Historical Society cookbook.

Makes 12 to 16 servings

4 cups chicken stock
2 cups long-grain white rice, uncooked
3 jars (6 ounces each) marinated artichoke hearts
5 green onions, chopped
1 jar (4 ounces) pimento-stuffed green olives, sliced
1 large green bell pepper, diced
3 ribs celery, diced
1/4 cup chopped fresh parsley
1 teaspoon curry powder
2 cups mayonnaise
Salt, to taste
Black pepper, to taste

In a large saucepan, bring chicken stock to a boil. Add rice; return to boiling. Reduce heat; cover and simmer 20 minutes, or until liquid is absorbed. Transfer to a large serving bowl; let cool.

Drain artichoke hearts, reserving marinade. Chop artichoke hearts. Add artichokes, green onions, olives, green pepper, celery and parsley to cooled rice.

For dressing, combine reserved artichoke marinade, curry powder and mayonnaise in a small bowl; mix well. Season to taste with salt and pepper.

Add dressing to rice mixture; mix thoroughly. Refrigerate until serving time.

Help others act responsibly about drinking and driving.

Couscous Salad with Radishes and Pine Nuts

Joanna Pruess
Free-Lance Writer, New York, NY

This refreshing combination of couscous, radishes and pine nuts, seasoned with orange juice and cilantro, is a distinctive side dish that complements roasted or grilled meats, poultry or fish.

Although most of the preparation for this salad can be done ahead of time, add the pine nuts and radishes just before serving so they are crisp and the radishes retain their bright red borders.

Makes 12 servings

1-1/2 cups chicken stock	1/4 to 1/3 cup vegetable oil
3 cups water	3 cups thinly sliced radishes
1 teaspoon salt	3/4 cup pine nuts (pignolia),
2 packages (10 ounces each)	toasted
quick-cooking couscous	1/4 cup cider vinegar
(3 cups uncooked couscous)	Salt, to taste
1-1/2 cups orange juice, divided	Freshly ground black pepper,
2 tablespoons grated orange peel	to taste
1 cup chopped fresh cilantro	

In a medium saucepan, bring chicken stock, water and salt to a boil. Add couscous in a slow, steady stream; stir until liquid has been absorbed. Turn off heat. Cover and let stand 2 minutes, or until couscous is tender.

Spread cooked couscous on a 15x10x1-inch baking sheet or other large container. Let cool 10 to 15 minutes. Separate clumps of couscous into individual grains by rubbing them between your palms or with a spatula.

When couscous is cool, transfer it to a large bowl. Add 1 cup orange juice, orange peel and cilantro; toss to blend.

Before serving, add oil, radishes, pine nuts, vinegar and remaining 1/2 cup orange juice; mix well. Season to taste with salt and pepper. Serve immediately.

Dill Potato Salad

Evelyn Cairns
Food Editor, *The News-Herald Newspapers*, Southgate, MI

It's not often that my husband, who has undergone heart bypass surgery and is on a special diet, is invited to a gathering at which heart-healthy foods are served. One exception was a recent potluck at the home of a friend. One nutrition-conscious guest contributed the recipe for this delicious dilled potato salad with a yogurt and light mayonnaise dressing. We all — but especially my husband — enjoyed it to our hearts' content!

Makes 6 to 8 servings

3 pounds potatoes
1 package (16 ounces)
    frozen peas
1/4 cup chopped onion
2 cloves garlic, minced
1 cup plain non-fat yogurt
1/3 cup light mayonnaise

1/2 teaspoon granulated sugar
1/2 teaspoon salt
1/4 teaspoon black pepper
1/4 teaspoon celery salt
2 teaspoons dried dill weed
2 tablespoons lemon juice

Boil potatoes in water to cover until tender. Let cool. Peel and slice thin.

Rinse frozen peas with hot water; drain well. Add peas to sliced potatoes. Add onion and garlic.

In a small bowl, combine yogurt, mayonnaise, sugar, salt, pepper, celery salt, dill weed and lemon juice; mix well. Pour over potato mixture; mix well. Refrigerate, covered, 4 hours to let flavors blend before serving.

Learn the facts about the dangers of drinking and driving.

Dockside Salad

Monetta L. Horr
Food Editor, *Jackson Citizen Patriot*, Jackson, MI

My friend Jo can make a party out of any occasion — or no occasion at all. Jo, who is nearing retirement, lives on a lake and nothing, absolutely nothing, rattles her gentle disposition. When she entertains, she makes mountains of food, and usually stops at the deli between town and the lake just to make sure she has enough. One evening, the party was to celebrate putting in her dock. Several men from her office, including my husband, were asked to help, while the wives supervised and the children swam and chased the ducks and geese. One of the dishes Jo bought for that evening was a spaghetti salad. We could figure out how the deli made the salad, except for the color. How did it get to be so red? I liked it so much that I finally stopped at the deli and asked. The woman who made the mouth-watering items in the deli case told me the surprise ingredient: paprika.

Makes 10 servings

1 package (16 ounces) spaghetti
2 green bell peppers, finely chopped
1 red bell pepper, finely chopped
1 large onion, finely chopped
1 bottle (16 ounces) zesty Italian salad dressing
Paprika

Cook spaghetti according to package directions; drain well.

In a large bowl, combine spaghetti, green peppers, red pepper and onion. Add Italian salad dressing; toss to coat spaghetti and vegetables. Sprinkle generously with paprika; stir well. Add more paprika to give mixture a red color. Stir again. Cover and refrigerate 4 hours or longer, stirring once or twice.

Garden Pasta Salad

Barbara Yost
Feature Writer, *The Phoenix Gazette*, Phoenix, AZ

My friend Ann Johnson gave me this recipe years ago. Many pasta salads served in restaurants look pretty but have little taste. This one, however, is tangy and contains enough ingredients that every one is bound to like something in it. For lunch, I like to serve this pasta salad with French bread, a few pieces of fruit and homemade lemonade.

Makes 6 servings

1 package (8 ounces) shell macaroni or rotini
1 tablespoon vegetable oil
1 jar (6 ounces) marinated artichoke hearts
1/2 cup Italian salad dressing
1 clove garlic, minced
2 tablespoons cider vinegar
1 cup mayonnaise

Salt, to taste
Black pepper, to taste
1/2 cup chopped, cooked broccoli
1/2 cup frozen peas, thawed
10 cherry tomatoes, halved
1/2 cup pitted, halved black olives

Cook pasta according to package directions, adding oil to cooking water. Drain well.

Put drained pasta in a large mixing bowl. Drain marinade from artichokes, pouring marinade over pasta. Add Italian salad dressing and garlic to pasta. Cut artichoke hearts into quarters; add to pasta. Gently mix.

In a small bowl, combine vinegar and mayonnaise. Season to taste with salt and pepper. Pour over pasta mixture. Gently stir in broccoli, peas, tomatoes and olives. Refrigerate overnight to let flavors blend. Mix gently before serving.

Recognize the signs of the alcohol-impaired driver.

Garnished Noodle Salad

Jeanne Voltz
Cookbook Author, Pittsboro, NC

Chinese chicken salad inspired this recipe. It is wildly Americanized, but the tang of sesame oil and fresh ginger is here. My friend Ruth Nesi serves a big bowl of cold dressed noodles with sliced turkey and sliced fresh tomatoes on hot summer days. In the winter, she garnishes the salad with orange slices and cucumber — refreshing and nourishing. You might think this is exotic, but this salad goes fast at church suppers.

Makes 6 to 8 servings

Soy-Vinegar Sauce:

1/4 cup soy sauce
1/4 cup red wine vinegar

2 tablespoons sesame oil
1 teaspoon granulated sugar

Salad:

1 pound thin fettucine or Chinese-style egg noodles, cooked and drained
2 tablespoons sesame oil or vegetable oil
1 tablespoon finely sliced fresh ginger
2 teaspoons minced garlic
2 tablespoons thinly sliced green onions (with tops)

2 teaspoons toasted sesame seeds
1-1/2 cups julienne-cut cooked turkey
1 cup coarsely shredded cucumber
1 cup orange segments or broken slices of orange
Leaf lettuce or Romaine lettuce
Radishes

For soy-vinegar sauce: Combine soy sauce, red wine vinegar, sesame oil and sugar. Mix well. Set aside.

For salad: Run cold water over freshly cooked and drained noodles. Drain again. Turn noodles into a large bowl; immediately toss with oil. Cover and let stand until ready to complete salad. Toss occasionally to prevent noodles from sticking together.

To complete salad, add ginger, garlic, green onions and sesame seeds to noodles; toss well. Add about 1/2 cup reserved soy-vinegar sauce; toss to coat noodles well. Place in large shallow bowl or on platter. Arrange turkey, cucumber and orange around noodle salad. Tuck greens around edges of salad and garnish with radishes. Drizzle more soy-vinegar sauce over salad when it is served.

Greek Salad

Teri M. Grimes
Assistant Features Editor, *The Bradenton Herald*, Bradenton, FL

Tarpon Springs, on Florida's west coast, was once the center of a thriving natural sponge industry, which attracted many Greek divers to settle there. It was here that I had my first taste of Greek food. The Louis Pappas Restaurant, which sits on the water's edge, serves a Greek salad that is justifiably famous. The secret is the potato salad.

Makes 4 servings

Potato Salad:

6 medium potatoes
2 medium onions, finely chopped
    (or 4 green onions,
    thinly sliced)
1/4 cup finely chopped fresh
    parsley

1/2 cup chopped green
    bell pepper
Salt, to taste
1/2 cup mayonnaise, or more
    if needed

Greek Salad:

1 large head iceberg lettuce
12 sprigs watercress or
    12 Greek roka leaves
2 tomatoes, cut into 6 wedges each
1 cucumber, peeled and cut
    lengthwise into 8 strips
1 avocado, peeled, pitted
    and cut into wedges
4 ounces feta cheese, sliced
1 green bell pepper, cut into
    8 rings
4 slices canned beets

4 shrimp, cooked and peeled
4 anchovy fillets
12 black Greek olives
12 medium-hot bottled Salonika
    peppers (or pepperoncinis)
4 radishes
4 green onions
1/2 cup white vinegar
1/4 cup olive oil
1/4 cup vegetable oil
Oregano, to taste

For potato salad: Boil unpeeled potatoes in water to cover 30 minutes, or until potatoes are tender but not soft. Drain, cool and peel potatoes. Slice potatoes into a large bowl. Add onions, parsley and green pepper to potatoes. Season lightly with salt. Fold in mayonnaise, using more if necessary to hold the salad together. You will need 3 cups potato salad for Greek Salad; refrigerate any extra potato salad for another use.

100 *Protect yourself from drunk drivers. Always wear your seat belt.*

For Greek salad: Line a large platter with the outside leaves of lettuce. Place 3 cups potato salad in a mound in the center of the platter. Shred remaining lettuce; use to cover potato salad. Arrange watercress on top of shredded lettuce.

Place tomato wedges around the outer edges of the salad and a few on top. Arrange cucumbers between tomatoes. Place avocado slices around outside edge of lettuce leaves. Arrange slices of feta cheese on top of salad. Scatter green pepper rings over all. On the very top, arrange sliced beets; top each beet slice with a shrimp and an anchovy fillet. Scatter olives, peppers, radishes and green onions over all.

Sprinkle vinegar over salad. Blend olive oil and vegetable oil; sprinkle over salad. Sprinkle oregano over all. Serve immediately.

Note: Serve toasted garlic bread with this salad.

Hot German Potato Salad

Sally Cappon
Food Columnist, *Santa Barbara News-Press*, Santa Barbara, CA

Growing up in Milwaukee where Hot German Potato Salad was a Sunday night staple, I had the job of going to Mr. Schreiber's delicatessen for a cardboard tub of the delicacy. Years later, a good friend, Sally Kroenke, gave me this recipe that matches my memories.

Makes 5 to 6 servings

5 medium to large potatoes	1 cup water
1/2 pound bacon, diced	1/2 cup granulated sugar
1 tablespoon all-purpose flour	1/4 cup chopped onion
1/2 cup cider vinegar	1/4 cup chopped celery

Cook potatoes in boiling water to cover 30 minutes, or until tender. Let cool; peel and slice. Place sliced potatoes in a serving bowl.

In a large skillet, fry bacon until crisp. Remove from heat. Remove bacon with a slotted spoon and drain on paper towels. Crumble bacon; add to potatoes.

Drain off all but about 1 tablespoon bacon grease. Stir flour into bacon grease in skillet. Gradually add vinegar and water, stirring constantly, to make a smooth mixture. Add sugar, onion and celery. Cook until sauce is hot and slightly thickened.

Pour hot sauce over potatoes and bacon; toss gently to coat. Serve hot.

Idaho's Greatest Potato Salad

Marie D. Galyean
Food Editor, *Idaho Press-Tribune*, Nampa, ID

After moving to the "Spud State" (Idaho), I thought I needed to come up with a special potato salad to do justice to our wonderful Idaho baking potatoes. According to my family, this is Idaho's Greatest Potato Salad. It's nothing fancy, but it allows the true flavor and texture of the potatoes to shine through, complemented by delicious flavors.

Makes 6 to 8 servings

4 to 6 medium or large potatoes, peeled and quartered
3 hard-cooked eggs, peeled, divided
1 medium onion, finely chopped
2 to 3 ribs celery, chopped
3 slices bacon, cooked crisp and crumbled

4 sweet pickle slices, chopped
1-1/2 teaspoons lime or lemon juice
2 teaspoons prepared mustard
1/4 teaspoon garlic powder
4 drops hot pepper sauce
1 to 1-1/2 cups mayonnaise
1/2 teaspoon paprika

The day before serving, or early in the morning, boil potatoes in water to cover 20 minutes, or until fork tender. Drain and let cool. When potatoes are at room temperature or cooler, dice potatoes into large or small chunks, as you prefer.

Put half the diced potatoes into a large serving bowl. Chop 2 of the hard-cooked eggs; add to potatoes in bowl. Stir in about one-half of these ingredients: onion, celery, bacon, pickle, lime juice, mustard, garlic powder, hot pepper sauce and mayonnaise. Mix well. Add remaining potatoes, onion, celery, bacon, pickle, lime juice, mustard, garlic powder, hot pepper sauce and mayonnaise. Mix well. Smooth the top of the salad.

Slice remaining 1 hard-cooked egg; place slices around the edge of the bowl. Lightly sprinkle paprika on top. Refrigerate, covered, until ready to serve.

Use proper car restraint systems for children under 5 years old.

Lancaster County Potato Salad

Frances Price
Columnist, *One and Only Cook*, Baltimore, MD

This recipe, which is right in tune with today's low-fat trend, was given to me by a good cook from Lancaster County some years ago, before dietary fat reared its ugly head. You'd never know from the rich taste and golden color that this Pennsylvania Dutch potato salad has less fat than regular potato salad made with mayonnaise, provided you leave out the crumbled bacon. The calorie-cutting secret is in the cooked dressing, which is made with water instead of oil.

Makes 10 to 12 servings

1/4 cup granulated sugar
1 tablespoon plus 1-1/2
    teaspoons all-purpose flour
1 teaspoon salt
3/4 cup hot water
1/4 cup cider vinegar
2 tablespoons bacon drippings or
    melted butter or margarine
1 egg, lightly beaten

2 teaspoons prepared mustard
2 tablespoons mayonnaise
4 pounds potatoes, cooked,
    peeled and thickly sliced
4 hard-cooked eggs, peeled and
    coarsely chopped
8 slices bacon, cooked crisp
    and crumbled

In a small saucepan, combine sugar, flour and salt until smooth. In a bowl, combine hot water, vinegar and bacon drippings; stir into sugar mixture. Stir in lightly beaten egg and mustard. Cook over medium-low heat, stirring constantly, until thickened. Remove from heat. Let cool to lukewarm. Stir in mayonnaise.

In a large mixing bowl, combine potato slices, hard-cooked eggs and crumbled bacon. Add dressing while it is still warm; toss gently to coat potatoes. Cover and refrigerate several hours before serving.

Serve chilled or warm. To serve warm, briefly reheat salad in a 350-degree oven or in a microwave oven.

Lentil Salad

Lorrie Guttman
Food Editor, *Tallahassee Democrat*, Tallahassee, FL

My friend Sally serves this lentil salad every year at her break-the-fast, the meal following the end of a day of fasting for Yom Kippur. She was generous enough to share the recipe, so now I can enjoy it year-round. The basil seems to be the seasoning that elevates this salad above the ordinary; you can use fresh or dried basil.

Makes 6 servings

1 small onion
2 whole cloves (or 1/4 teaspoon ground cloves)
2/3 cup lentils, uncooked, rinsed
1 bay leaf
1/2 teaspoon salt
2 cups water
3 medium tomatoes, chopped
6 green onions, thinly sliced
1/3 cup finely chopped fresh parsley, divided

1 tablespoon chopped fresh basil (or 1 teaspoon dried basil crumbled)
3 tablespoons olive oil
1 tablespoon lemon juice
1 tablespoon balsamic vinegar or red wine vinegar
Salt, to taste
Freshly ground black pepper, to taste

Pierce onion with whole cloves. (Or, if using ground cloves, add to water along with other ingredients.) In a large saucepan, combine clove-studded onion, lentils, bay leaf, 1/2 teaspoon salt and water. Bring to a boil, then reduce heat. Cover and simmer 25 minutes, or until lentils are tender. Drain lentils; remove and discard onion and bay leaf.

In a large glass or ceramic bowl, gently toss lentils, tomatoes, green onions, half the parsley and the basil.

In a small bowl, whisk together oil, lemon juice and vinegar. Pour over lentil mixture. Season to taste with salt and pepper. Gently toss to thoroughly combine.

Garnish with remaining parsley. Serve slightly chilled or at room temperature.

Macaroni Salad, Creole Style

Frances Price
Columnist, *One and Only Cook*, Baltimore, MD

> *This salad was a childhood favorite of mine. It later became a favorite of my daughters. Mother clipped the original recipe from Mrs. S. R. Dull's column in the Atlanta Journal. She made it early in the day in the summer. (In those pre-air-conditioned days, it was generally too hot to cook in the late afternoon.) This salad is, to my way of thinking, the best of all possible macaroni salads. In fact, I could eat the whole thing, right now!*

Makes 4 to 6 servings

1 package (8 ounces) elbow macaroni

1 ripe tomato, cut into 1/2-inch cubes

1 cup coarsely grated Cheddar cheese (4 ounces)

1 medium carrot, peeled and grated

1 cup finely chopped celery

1/2 cup finely chopped green or red bell pepper

1/3 cup sliced pimento-stuffed green olives

2 tablespoons finely chopped red onion

1 cup mayonnaise

2 tablespoons cider vinegar

Salt, to taste

Black pepper, to taste

Cook macaroni according to package directions.

While macaroni cooks, combine tomato, cheese, carrot, celery, green pepper, olives and onion in a large mixing bowl. Stir in mayonnaise and vinegar.

When macaroni tests done, immediately set pan under cold running water to stop the cooking. Drain, rinse under cold water, drain again.

Add macaroni to tomato mixture. Toss gently to mix. Season to taste with salt and pepper. Cover and refrigerate several hours or overnight, to let flavors blend.

Muscovite Potato Salad

Jim Hillibish
Food Editor, *The Repository*, Canton, OH

Potatoes, earthy and sweet, are a table staple in Russia. Finding ways to end their monotony is a national pastime in the U.S.S.R. This recipe is from a Russian immigrant who became an American citizen in Ohio after leaving his native Moscow soon after World War II. He insists its success is based on finding new, red potatoes — those small fruits of the first harvest valued everywhere for their tenderness and flavor.

Makes 4 servings

2 tablespoons white vinegar
2 tablespoons cider vinegar
1 tablespoon brown sugar
1 teaspoon salt
1 teaspoon coarse-grain mustard
1 cup peeled, seeded and
    diced cucumber

2 cups plain yogurt
1 cup dairy sour cream
1 tablespoon fresh lemon juice
1 tablespoon dried dill weed
8 medium-size new, red potatoes,
    unpeeled
Freshly ground black pepper

In a large non-metallic bowl, combine white vinegar, cider vinegar, brown sugar, salt, mustard, cucumber, yogurt, sour cream, lemon juice and dill. Mix well. Cover and refrigerate while preparing potatoes.

Gently scrub potatoes with a brush, being careful not to damage the skins. Put potatoes in a large saucepan; cover with water and bring to a boil; cook over medium-high heat 10 to 15 minutes, or until fork tender. Cool potatoes under cold running water; drain. Cut each potato into quarters.

Fold potatoes into yogurt mixture with a wooden spoon, being careful not to bruise the potatoes. Refrigerate for at least 6 hours to let flavors blend. Season with pepper before serving.

Note: This salad will keep up to three days in the refrigerator.

About 1 out of 25 drivers is legally drunk on a weekday night.

No-Sweat New Potato Salad

Paul Grondahl
Feature Writer, *Albany Times Union*, Albany, NY

*If you tend to procrastinate when invited to a summer potluck picnic —
like myself and most other food writers I know — you'll appreciate the
special absolution from obligatory peeling granted by using new potatoes. No more skinned knuckles before the softball game. No more
cursing over the potato peeler on a hot August afternoon. And we all
learned from our mothers that all the nutrients are in the potato skin
anyway, right? Why, then, do most potato salad recipes call for throwing
out the good stuff? So, use the delicate little blushing spuds in this twist
on an American classic and your friends won't think you were just saving
time, they'll think you're a trendy gourmand.*

Makes 16 to 20 servings

4 pounds new potatoes
1/2 cup red wine vinegar
1/4 cup extra-virgin olive oil
1/2 teaspoon freshly ground
   black pepper
1/2 cup finely chopped red onion

1 cup chopped celery
1/2 cup chopped fresh parsley
2-1/2 cups mayonnaise
1/4 cup Dijon-style mustard
5 hard-cooked eggs, peeled
   and sliced thin

Wash and gently scrub new potatoes. Add unpeeled potatoes to a pot
of boiling water. Cook 15 minutes, or until potatoes are tender yet still firm.
Drain potatoes. Cut potatoes into quarters and place in a large mixing bowl.

While potatoes are still warm, sprinkle them with vinegar and olive oil.
Add pepper, red onion, celery, parsley, mayonnaise and mustard. Mix well.
Add about half of the sliced hard-cooked eggs; mix gently. Use remaining
sliced eggs as garnish. Let the salad cool, then cover and refrigerate it a few
hours or overnight.

Orzo Salad

Jane Witty Gould
Lifestyle Copy Editor, *The Courier-News*, Bridgewater, NJ

This recipe was given to me by a friend from Philadelphia who tasted it at one of her favorite restaurants, The Frog Commissary. As the recipe was passed along, it invariably went through some changes. I reduced the amount of vegetable oil because it was a little too slippery for my family's taste. This pasta salad with its subtle sesame-orange-ginger flavor is the perfect foil for everything from grilled flank steak to butterflied leg of lamb.

Makes 6 to 8 servings

1 teaspoon salt
1/2 cup vegetable oil
3 tablespoons sesame oil, divided
1/2 cup rice vinegar
1 tablespoon sherry vinegar
1/2 teaspoon grated orange peel
1 teaspoon soy sauce
2 tablespoons thinly sliced
    green onions
1 teaspoon minced fresh ginger
1/2 teaspoon minced garlic
1/4 teaspoon crushed red
    pepper flakes

1 teaspoon freshly ground
    black pepper
1 tablespoon granulated sugar
2 tablespoons chopped fresh
    cilantro or parsley
1 package (16 ounces) orzo
    (rice-shaped pasta)
3 cups shredded carrots
2 cups raisins
3/4 cup pine nuts (pignolia),
    lightly toasted

In a mixing bowl, combine salt, vegetable oil, 2 tablespoons sesame oil, rice vinegar, sherry vinegar, orange peel, soy sauce, green onions, ginger, garlic, red pepper flakes, pepper, sugar and cilantro. Mix well. Reserve.

Cook orzo according to package directions. Refresh under cold water. Drain well. Place orzo in a glass serving bowl. Toss with remaining 1 tablespoon sesame oil. Let cool completely.

Add carrots, raisins, pine nuts and reserved oil mixture to orzo. Gently mix. Refrigerate, covered, until serving time.

Note: This salad can be prepared one day ahead, but don't add carrots and pine nuts until just before serving, so they will remain crunchy.

69% of all drivers killed in single-vehicle crashes in 1990 had a BAC of .10 or more.

Pecos Pasta Salad

Toni Burks
Food Editor, *Roanoke Times & World-News*, Roanoke, VA

In the beginning, there was macaroni salad. Today, it's pasta salad. In either, anything goes. For our neighborhood Fourth of July picnic one year, I tossed everything but the kitchen sink into a big bowl of multi-colored spiral pasta. The result was a salad with a definite Southwestern drawl.

Makes 6 to 8 servings

4 cups cooked multi-colored spiral pasta, rinsed in cold water and drained
1 cup sliced green onions
2 cups diced tomato
1 can (4 ounces) chopped green chilies, drained
1/2 cup pitted, sliced black olives
1 cup frozen corn kernels, thawed
2 tablespoons chopped fresh cilantro or parsley
2 tablespoons lime juice
2/3 cup bottled medium-hot picante sauce or salsa
Mayonnaise

In large salad bowl, combine pasta, green onions, tomato, chilies, olives, corn, cilantro, lime juice and picante sauce. Stir to blend well. Add enough mayonnaise to coat salad ingredients well. Refrigerate to let flavors blend before serving.

Tabbouleh

Delmer Robinson
Food Editor, *The Charleston Gazette*, Charleston, WV

From the Middle East to the mountains of West Virginia, this has to be one of the most cooling and refreshing salads of summertime. Charleston has a large Syrian-Lebanese population and Tabbouleh is always served at fund-raising ethnic dinners for their church.

Makes 6 servings

1 cup bulghur wheat (fine)
6 to 8 green onions, finely chopped
1-1/2 cups finely chopped fresh parsley
1/4 to 1/2 cup finely chopped fresh mint

3 large tomatoes, finely chopped
Juice of 3 lemons
1/3 cup olive oil
Salt, to taste
Black pepper, to taste
Lettuce leaves

Soak bulghur in water to cover for 1 hour. Squeeze dry by pressing between palms.

In a large salad bowl, combine bulghur, green onions, parsley, mint and tomatoes; mix well. Stir in lemon juice, oil, salt and pepper; mix well. Serve with large lettuce leaves to use as scoops.

Note: Use plenty of lemon juice; the salad should be quite tart.

Remember that drunk drivers can strike anyone, at any time.

Wild Rice Salad

Jane Witty Gould
Lifestyle Copy Editor, *The Courier-News*, Bridgewater, NJ

One summer, not long after cold pasta salads became popular, I was searching for a similar type of recipe for wild rice. Although recipes abounded for white rice salads, few capitalized on the nutty taste and texture of wild rice. Ultimately, I developed my own recipe which makes an elegant accompaniment to grilled duck, salmon or fillet of beef.

Makes 6 servings

1 cup wild rice, uncooked
3 cups water
Salt, to taste
1 tablespoon extra-virgin olive oil
Freshly ground black pepper,
    to taste
1/2 cup sliced green onions
    (1/4-inch pieces;
    green part only)

1/4 cup toasted pine nuts
    (pignolia)
Juice of 1/2 lemon
1 large yellow bell pepper,
    sliced into thin rings
6 cherry tomatoes, halved
    crosswise
1/4 cup minced fresh parsley

Rinse rice under cold running water. Bring 3 cups water to a boil in a large saucepan. Add salt to taste. Add rice. Return to boiling. Reduce heat, cover and simmer 40 minutes. (After 20 minutes, taste every 5 minutes. Rice grains should pop open to reveal the white insides but should not turn mushy.)

Drain in colander. Dry rice on paper towels. Turn into an attractive glass serving bowl. Toss with olive oil. Season to taste with salt and pepper. Add green onions; toss with a fork. Scatter pine nuts on top. Let stand, loosely covered, at room temperature 2 hours before serving.

Just before serving, squeeze lemon juice over salad; toss gently. Garnish with yellow pepper rings and cherry tomato halves. Sprinkle parsley over all.

Yellow Rice Salad

Sally Scherer
Food Writer, *The Macon Telegraph*, Macon, GA

Yellow rice is always delicious. This recipe with water chestnuts and artichokes makes it even more so. A former neighbor gave me this recipe. She served it at family get-togethers, where the recipe was requested by almost everyone.

Makes 10 servings

1 package (10 ounces) yellow rice
4 to 6 green onions, chopped, including tops
24 pimento-stuffed green olives, sliced
1 can (8 ounces) sliced water chestnuts, drained
1/2 to 3/4 teaspoon curry powder
1/2 teaspoon salt
1/2 teaspoon dried dill weed
1/8 teaspoon black pepper
2 jars (6 ounces each) marinated artichoke hearts
1/2 cup mayonnaise
Lettuce

Cook rice according to package directions. Add green onions, olives and water chestnuts. Mix well. Add curry powder, salt, dill weed and pepper.

Drain artichokes, reserving marinade. Cut artichokes into quarters; stir into rice mixture. Mix reserved artichoke marinade with mayonnaise; toss with rice mixture. Refrigerate overnight to let flavors blend. Serve on lettuce leaves.

The average arrested drunk driver consumed 6 ounces of pure alcohol in 4 hours.

SEAFOOD, POULTRY &MEAT SALADS

Chicken and Goat Cheese Salad

Lori Longbotham
Free-Lance Food Writer, New York, NY

This is a French-inspired entrée salad that is perfect for summertime al fresco dining. Just add a frosty glass of iced tea and a loaf of crusty bread for a delightful meal. Walnut oil adds a lovely flavor, but if you don't have it, use olive oil.

Makes 6 servings

1 cup walnut oil or olive oil
3 sprigs fresh parsley
3 sprigs fresh thyme
1 bay leaf
1 clove garlic, crushed
10 black peppercorns, crushed
1 log (11 ounces) Montrachet goat cheese, cut crosswise into 12 slices
1 bunch arugula
3 bunches watercress
3 Belgian endives
1/4 cup ground walnuts
1/2 cup dry bread crumbs

24 walnut halves
1 green onion, minced
1/4 cup fresh lemon juice
1 tablespoon imported coarse-grain mustard
1 teaspoon Dijon-style mustard
1/4 teaspoon salt
1/8 teaspoon freshly ground black pepper
3 smoked chicken breasts, skinned, boned and sliced on the diagonal
1 small zucchini, julienned
18 Nicoise olives

In a medium bowl, combine oil, parsley, thyme, bay leaf, garlic and peppercorns. Add goat cheese; let marinate 1 hour.

Rinse and drain arugula, watercress and endives. Remove and discard large stems from arugula and watercress. Tear arugula, watercress and endives into bite-size pieces; toss together in a large bowl. Refrigerate until ready to serve.

In a small bowl, combine ground walnuts and bread crumbs. Drain cheese; strain marinade and reserve. Coat cheese slices with walnut-crumb mixture. Place on a non-stick baking sheet. Bake in a preheated 350-degree oven 12 minutes, or until warmed through.

Meanwhile, toast walnut halves in a non-stick skillet over medium heat until fragrant.

6 ounces of pure alcohol is equal to 12 bottles of beer or 8 mixed drinks.

In a small bowl, combine reserved marinade, green onion, lemon juice, coarse-grain mustard, Dijon mustard, salt and pepper; mix well. Pour dressing over greens and toss to coat. Divide greens among six large salad plates.

Arrange chicken, zucchini, walnut halves, olives and warm cheese slices on greens. Serve immediately.

Couscous Chicken Salad

Goody L. Solomon
Free-Lance Writer, Washington, D. C.

To prepare everyday meals, I often have to set aside time in late evenings or weekends to prepare foods that can be brought to the table with little additional fuss. That means substantial, robust salads as the main course. Here's one that makes a splendid meal with a loaf of good bread.

Makes 4 servings

1-1/4 cups chicken broth	Freshly ground black pepper, to taste
1 cup uncooked couscous	
1 tablespoon margarine	1 cup cooked, diced chicken
3/4 cup olive oil	4 large green onions, diced
3 tablespoons fresh lemon juice	1 large crisp apple, cored and diced
1 teaspoon salt	
1/2 teaspoon ground coriander	1 large rib celery, diced
1/2 teaspoon Dijon-style mustard	Lettuce leaves
1 large clove garlic, minced	Parsley sprigs, for garnish

In a saucepan, bring chicken broth to a boil. Add couscous and margarine. Bring to a boil again; cover, remove from heat and let stand 5 minutes. Fluff couscous with a fork and let cool. You should have about 2 cups cooked couscous.

In a small bowl, combine olive oil, lemon juice, salt, coriander, mustard, garlic and pepper; mix well.

In a large bowl, combine cooled couscous, chicken, green onions, apple and celery. Add olive oil mixture; toss to coat all ingredients.

Serve on a bed of lettuce. Garnish with parsley. Season to taste with freshly ground black pepper.

Couscous Salad with Shrimp and Oranges

Caroline Stuart
Contributing Editor, *Hudson Valley Magazine*, Poughkeepsie, NY

Couscous is a staple in North African cuisine where it is cooked and served as a porridge, with meat as a main course, as salad, or with fruit as a dessert. As a salad, it makes great picnic or party fare and can be prepared in advance. This couscous salad is light, economical and a snap to prepare. The oranges and raisins make an appealing flavor combination and the shrimp adds just the right contrast. Packaged couscous is available is most supermarkets and specialty food stores.

Makes 4 servings

1 large orange
1 cup cooked and peeled
  large shrimp
1 cup uncooked couscous
1-1/2 cups orange juice
1/4 cup vegetable oil
2 teaspoons fresh lemon juice

1 tablespoon grated fresh ginger
1 tablespoon grated orange peel
3 tablespoons raisins
1/4 cup chopped walnuts, toasted
1/4 cup finely chopped
  fresh parsley

Peel orange; remove white pith and membrane. Cut into segments. Reserve a few whole segments for garnish. Halve remaining segments.

Reserve a few whole shrimp for garnish. Cut remaining shrimp into bite-sized pieces.

Cook the couscous according to package directions, substituting orange juice for water as the cooking liquid. When cooked, transfer couscous to a bowl and fluff with a fork, separating any lumps. Drizzle oil and lemon juice over couscous; continue to fluff the grains. Add ginger, orange peel, halved orange segments, raisins, walnuts, parsley and cut-up shrimp. Mix well. Refrigerate several hours before serving.

Just before serving, toss lightly. Garnish with reserved whole shrimp and reserved whole orange segments.

Note: To toast walnuts, spread them in a shallow pan. Bake in a preheated 300-degree oven 10 minutes, stirring often to prevent burning.

Drunk driving is the most frequently committed violent crime in America.

Grilled Chicken Salad

Jeanne Delia
Food Columnist, *The Sun News*, Myrtle Beach, SC

To perk up my family's appetites during the hot days of summer, I serve a grilled salad. This recipe was inspired by a salad I tasted during a trip to New Haven, Connecticut. It was an outstanding grilled chicken salad, dressed with a raspberry-balsamic vinaigrette and shavings of Gorgonzola, an Italian blue-veined cheese. After several attempts, I finally created a version that my family loves.

Makes 4 servings

4 chicken breast halves
    (about 4 ounces each)
Salt, to taste
Black pepper, to taste
Olive oil
2 bunches arugula or watercress
2 tablespoons balsamic vinegar

1 teaspoon Dijon-style mustard
6 tablespoons olive oil
1 cup frozen raspberries with
    syrup, slightly thawed
Grated Gorgonzola or
    blue cheese

Rinse chicken breast halves in cold water; pat dry. Skin and bone chicken. Season with salt and pepper; rub with olive oil. Put on oiled grill, meaty-side down. Grill over medium heat 5 minutes, then turn half-way to obtain crisscross grid marks and cook about 5 minutes more. Turn pieces over and grill 8 minutes, or until no longer pink inside.

While chicken is cooking, rinse and drain arugula; pat dry. Arrange arugula on 4 large salad plates.

In a medium bowl, combine vinegar and mustard; whisk in 6 table-spoons olive oil. Season to taste with salt and pepper. Just before serving, stir in raspberries with syrup.

Remove chicken from grill; cut into finger-sized pieces. Fan out pieces on one side of each plate. Drizzle dressing along bottom edges of chicken. Sprinkle cheese over all.

Note: If desired, garnish plates with sliced melon and grapes. For dinner or lunch, serve with Italian bread. For brunch, serve with assorted hot muffins.

Ham Salad with Hot Peanut Dressing

Clara Eschmann
Food Editor (retired), *The Macon Telegraph and News*, Macon, GA

Although I am no longer a full-time food editor, I write a weekly column for the newspaper and receive numerous recipes from a variety of sources. I often try out ones that appeal to me. When this salad recipe arrived, it received immediate attention. That's because ham is a favorite in my family, and my son is a peanut farmer in southwest Georgia.

Makes 6 servings

3/4 pound boneless, cooked ham
2 tablespoons peanut oil
   (or vegetable oil)
1/4 cup peanut butter
3 tablespoons fresh lime juice
1 tablespoon reduced-sodium
   soy sauce
1 teaspoon ground ginger
1 clove garlic, minced

1 tablespoon granulated sugar
1 medium cucumber, seeded
   and thinly sliced
1 small red onion, thinly sliced
6 cups torn Romaine lettuce or
   curly endive (bite-size pieces)
1 head radicchio or Boston lettuce
1/2 cup dry-roasted peanuts
   (optional)

Thinly slice ham. Heat briefly in microwave oven or in a skillet over medium heat. Keep warm.

Combine oil, peanut butter, lime juice, soy sauce, ginger, garlic and sugar in electric blender or food processor. Blend well. Pour peanut butter mixture into a glass measuring cup or small saucepan; heat in a microwave oven or on top of the stove until mixture is hot and bubbly.

In a large bowl, combine cucumber, onion and Romaine lettuce or endive.

Line individual serving plates or a large salad bowl with radicchio; top with cucumber mixture. Arrange equal portions of ham over each serving. Spoon hot peanut dressing over ham. Sprinkle peanuts on top, if desired.

Only 1 out of every 2,000 drunk drivers is ever arrested.

Hot Chicken Salad

June Ann Gladfelter
Managing Editor/Features, *The Express*, Easton, PA

My mother, Minnie Gladfelter, used to run off copies of this recipe because she got so many requests for it. When my brother was married, we served this as a specialty of the groom's family (the rest of the meal was catered). It is good served hot or cold. It also can be frozen to have on hand for special occasions and emergencies.

Makes 6 servings

2 cups cooked, chopped chicken (bite-size pieces)	2 tablespoons grated onion
	2 tablespoons lemon juice
1 to 2 cups finely chopped celery	3/4 cup mayonnaise
1/2 cup toasted slivered almonds	1/2 cup grated Cheddar cheese
1/2 teaspoon salt	1 to 2 cups crushed potato chips

In a large mixing bowl, combine chicken, celery, almonds, salt, onion, lemon juice and mayonnaise. Mix well. Transfer to a lightly greased 1-1/2-quart baking dish. Top with cheese and potato chips. Bake in a preheated 425-degree oven 10 minutes, or until hot and bubbly.

Note: This salad can be made ahead and refrigerated or frozen before baking. The frozen casserole should be thawed before baking as directed in recipe, or the frozen (unthawed) casserole can be baked in a preheated 350-degree oven 30 minutes, or until hot and bubbly.

King Gasparilla XLVII Salad

Mary D. Scourtes
Food Writer, *The Tampa Tribune*, Tampa, FL

This recipe was created long before the words cholesterol and saturated fat made it into everyday vocabulary. Named for the Gasparilla Invasion in Tampa every February, this salad was developed by my neighbor Jim Ferman, who was king of the celebration many years ago.

Makes 12 servings

2 large heads iceberg lettuce, cored, rinsed and shredded
3 ribs celery, finely chopped
1/2 cup finely chopped salted peanuts
4 slices bacon, cooked crisp and crumbled

1 jar (2-1/2 ounces) dried beef, finely shredded
1/2 cup chopped carrots
1 bottle (8 ounces) blue cheese salad dressing

In a large bowl, combine lettuce, celery, peanuts, bacon, beef and carrots. Mix well. Toss with blue cheese dressing. Serve immediately.

King Ranch Chicken Salad

Beth Whitley Duke
Food Editor, *Amarillo Globe-News*, Amarillo, TX

This recipe combines two regional favorites: Hot Chicken Salad and King Ranch Chicken Casserole. This blend of flavors makes a savory salad that can stand double duty as a main dish at dinner.

Makes 6 to 8 servings

6 chicken breasts, cooked, skinned, boned and chopped
1 medium onion, chopped
1 can (4 ounces) chopped green chilies, drained
1 can (4-1/2 ounces) chopped black olives, drained
1 cup mayonnaise

1 cup dairy sour cream
2 cups crushed tortilla chips, divided
1 cup grated Monterey Jack cheese
1 cup grated sharp Colby or Cheddar cheese

A .02 BAC can impair driving abilities and increase the chances of a crash.

In a large mixing bowl, combine chicken, onion, chilies, olives, mayonnaise and sour cream. Add 1 cup tortilla chips; mix well.

Spread half the chicken mixture in a greased 13x9x2-inch baking pan. Sprinkle Monterey Jack cheese over chicken mixture in pan. Spread remaining chicken mixture over cheese. Cover chicken mixture with Colby cheese. Top with remaining 1 cup tortilla chips. Bake in a preheated 400-degree oven 10 minutes, or until hot and bubbly.

Layered Mexican Club Salad

Arlene Christianson Pickard
Free-Lance Food Writer, Portland, OR

When recipes for layered salad were introduced, I loved the idea but not the peas. So I created a no-pea layered salad, using the flavor combinations from the traditional club sandwich, plus salsa and cumin for a Mexican touch. I also added bell peppers, which are available in a rainbow of colors in Oregon. In line with current trends, I use low-salt bacon and reduced-calorie mayonnaise.

Makes 4 to 6 servings

1 package (12 ounces) low-salt
    bacon, cooked, drained
    and crumbled
1 can (2-1/4 ounces) sliced
    black olives, drained
1 cup reduced-calorie
    mayonnaise
1/2 cup salsa
1-1/2 teaspoons ground cumin
6 cups shredded lettuce

2 large tomatoes, chopped
6 to 8 green onions, sliced
1-1/2 cups cooked, chopped
    chicken or turkey
1 large green, red or yellow
    bell pepper
1 small sourdough roll
    (3 to 4 ounces), cubed
1 avocado, peeled and
    sliced (optional)

In a mixing bowl, combine bacon, olives, mayonnaise, salsa and cumin. Mix well.

In a 3- to 4-quart, clear, straight-sided salad bowl, layer lettuce, tomatoes, green onions, chicken, bell pepper and bread cubes. Spread half the bacon dressing over top layer. Cover and refrigerate salad several hours or overnight. Cover and refrigerate remaining bacon dressing.

Just before serving, garnish salad with avocado slices, if desired. Pass remaining bacon dressing at the table.

Lamb Salad

Doris Reynolds
Food Columnist, *Naples Daily News*, Naples, FL

I first tasted lamb salad at La Cirque in New York City. The chef would not part with the recipe, so I experimented and came up with this creation. Although it is quite different than the La Cirque recipe, it has received rave reviews from friends and family. Even those who do not particularly like lamb find this warm salad appetizing.

Makes 6 servings

1-1/2 pounds lean lamb, cut into 2-inch strips
1 cup extra-virgin olive oil
1/2 cup red wine vinegar
5 cloves garlic (more or less, depending on taste), crushed
Kosher salt, to taste
Freshly ground black pepper, to taste
1/2 cup walnut halves
6 cups mixed salad greens (arugula, watercress, Bibb, and/or Boston lettuce)
Asparagus, radishes and/or endive, for garnish

About two or three hours ahead of time (or the night before), combine lamb, olive oil, vinegar, garlic, salt and pepper in a non-metallic bowl. Let marinate in refrigerator, turning lamb strips occasionally.

Drain lamb, reserving marinade. In a skillet, heat marinade to boiling. Add lamb, stirring constantly. Cook 10 minutes, or until lamb is done as desired. Remove from heat. Add walnuts; mix well. Adjust seasonings to taste.

Divide salad greens among 6 salad plates; place warm lamb mixture on greens. Garnish with asparagus, radishes and/or endive, if desired.

At a .08 BAC, your risk of being in a crash is 3 to 4 times greater than when sober.

Magnolia Salmon Mousse

Carolyn Flournoy
Food Columnist, *The Times*, Shreveport, LA

In Louisiana, we are blessed with a largesse of seafood — shrimp, crab, crawfish, red snapper, to name a few. However, no self-respecting Magnolia State buffet would be complete without a salmon dish. It is a must at Mardi Gras parties and holiday festivities. I adapted this recipe from a shrimp mousse recipe and find it twice as good as the original.

Makes 8 entrée servings; 12 to 15 buffet servings

1 can (16 ounces) red sockeye
  salmon, drained
3 tablespoons lemon juice
1 cup dairy sour cream
1 package (8 ounces) cream
  cheese, softened
1/2 cup mayonnaise
1/4 cup chili sauce
1/4 teaspoon hot pepper sauce
2 teaspoons Worcestershire sauce
1/2 teaspoon salt

1/2 teaspoon white pepper
2 envelopes unflavored gelatin
1/4 cup cold water
1/2 cup boiling water
1/2 cup finely chopped green
  bell pepper
1/2 cup finely chopped celery
1/2 cup finely chopped green
  onions
Parsley sprigs, for garnish

Pick over salmon, removing skin and bones. Sprinkle salmon with lemon juice. Set aside.

In a food processor or with an electric mixer, combine sour cream, cream cheese and mayonnaise. Add chili sauce, hot pepper sauce, Worcestershire sauce, salt and white pepper; mix well.

Meanwhile, soften gelatin in cold water, then add boiling water; stir to dissolve gelatin. Let cool, then add to cream cheese mixture in food processor; mix well. Add salmon; process just until mixtures are combined. Fold in bell pepper, celery and green onions.

Pour into a greased 2-quart mold. Refrigerate, covered, overnight. Unmold and garnish with parsley.

Mango and Ginger Chicken Salad

Mary Beth Jung
Free-Lance Writer, Grafton, WI

This refreshing main-course salad is quick to prepare and oh, so satisfying. I developed the recipe several years ago when I was given several ripe mangos. The ginger adds a delightful tang to this combination of sweet, savory and crunchy. It is best to prepare this salad several hours before serving to allow flavors to blend.

Makes 4 to 6 servings

2 tablespoons vegetable oil
1 teaspoon grated fresh ginger
1 clove garlic, minced
1 pound boneless chicken or
    turkey breast, cut into
    1-inch cubes
Salt, to taste
Black pepper, to taste
1/4 cup chicken broth

1 tablespoon fresh lemon juice
1/4 cup regular or light
    mayonnaise
1/4 cup plain yogurt
1 mango, peeled and diced
1/2 cup diced celery
1/4 cup minced red bell pepper
Thinly sliced green onions,
    for garnish

In a skillet, heat the oil. Add ginger, garlic, chicken, salt and pepper; sauté 3 to 4 minutes, or until chicken is cooked. Remove chicken to salad bowl.

Add chicken broth and lemon juice to mixture remaining in skillet. Boil to reduce pan liquid to about 1 tablespoon, scraping brown bits from skillet. Let cool.

In a bowl, combine reduced pan liquid, mayonnaise and yogurt. Toss with chicken. Add mango, celery and red pepper; mix well. Refrigerate several hours before serving. Garnish with green onions.

You have a 40% chance of being in an alcohol-related crash during your lifetime.

Maurice Salad

Evelyn Cairns
Food Editor, *The News-Herald Newspapers*, Southgate, MI

"It's a closely guarded secret," I was told when I called the restaurant at Hudson's, a department store chain, to ask for their Maurice Salad recipe on behalf of a reader. I reported my failure to my readers — and the next week I received eight different versions of the "secret" recipe from women who had worked in the restaurant or knew someone who had. Each claimed her recipe was the real thing! The following version came closest to the salad I have enjoyed many times. It is one of the most popular menu items at the stores' restaurants.

Makes 6 servings

2 cups mayonnaise
3 hard-cooked egg yolks, grated
3 tablespoons grated onion
2 tablespoons finely chopped
fresh parsley
4 to 5 cups shredded lettuce

2 cups boiled, julienned ham
2 cups cooked, julienned chicken
or turkey breast
2 cups julienned Swiss cheese
12 sweet gherkins, thinly sliced

In a small bowl, combine mayonnaise, egg yolks, onion and parsley; mix well. Cover and refrigerate several hours to let flavors blend.

In a large serving bowl, toss together lettuce, ham, chicken, cheese and gherkins. Pour some of the mayonnaise mixture over lettuce mixture; toss to coat all ingredients. Pass remaining mayonnaise mixture at the table.

Mediterranean Tuna-Cannellini Salad

Miriam Morgan
Food Editor, *San Mateo Times*, San Mateo, CA

Lots of basil and capers give this Mediterranean-style tuna and white bean salad punch and verve. Make the dressing ahead of time to allow flavors to blend. Serve the salad at room temperature for lunch or for a no-cook dinner on a warm summer evening. It's also a great contribution to a potluck gathering.

Makes 4 to 6 servings

Dressing:

4 tablespoons capers
5 tablespoons red wine vinegar
1 tablespoon balsamic vinegar
(or another tablespoon
red wine vinegar)
1/2 teaspoon crushed
garlic (2 cloves)

1/4 teaspoon salt
1/4 teaspoon freshly ground
black pepper
3 to 4 tablespoons extra-virgin
olive oil

Salad:

2 cans (6-1/2 to 7 ounces each)
solid white or light water-pack
tuna, drained and flaked
1/3 cup chopped red or
green onion
4 medium tomatoes, chopped
1/2 cup chopped fresh basil
2 tablespoons minced fresh
parsley

2 cans (15 ounces each)
cannellini beans (white
kidney beans), rinsed and
well drained (or 4 cups
cooked small white
beans, drained)
Romaine lettuce or fresh
spinach leaves (optional)

For dressing: In a container with a tight-fitting lid, combine capers, red wine vinegar, balsamic vinegar, garlic, salt, pepper and oil. Cover and shake well; set aside 1 to 2 hours to let flavors blend (refrigerate, if prepared a day or several hours ahead).

For salad: In a large serving bowl, combine tuna, onion, tomatoes, basil, parsley and beans. Mix well. Refrigerate, if not serving right away.

Just before serving, pour dressing over tuna mixture. Toss gently to combine. Serve over lettuce or spinach leaves, if desired.

MADD is working to reduce drunk driving deaths another 20% by the year 2000.

Mussel, Potato and Asparagus Salad

Joanna Pruess
Free-Lance Writer, New York, NY

This recipe was inspired by a warm potato and asparagus salad I had at the home of friends in Paris. Once back in the United States, I enhanced the combination by adding another of my favorite foods: mussels. Now, I serve this as a main course on warm summer evenings. It's kind of addictive.

Makes 6 to 8 servings

2 pounds new red potatoes, scrubbed

1/4 teaspoon coarse or kosher salt

3 large shallots, peeled and finely chopped

3/4 cup finely chopped fresh parsley

2 tablespoons red wine vinegar

1 cup mayonnaise

1 tablespoon Dijon-style mustard

3 tablespoons small capers, drained

Salt, to taste

Freshly ground black pepper, to taste

3 pounds mussels, steamed and shelled (about 1 pound mussel flesh)

3/4 pound thin asparagus spears, steamed until crisp-tender, and cut into 1-inch pieces

Chopped fresh parsley, for garnish

In a large saucepot, cover potatoes with water; bring to a boil. Add salt. Reduce heat; simmer 12 to 14 minutes, or until potatoes are fork tender. Drain; let cool.

In a medium bowl, combine shallots, parsley, vinegar, mayonnaise and mustard; mix well. Fold in capers. Season to taste with salt and pepper.

Cut potatoes into cubes; put into a large bowl. Add about three-fourths of the shallot dressing. Toss to coat potatoes.

Just before serving, add mussels, asparagus and remaining shallot dressing to potato mixture; toss again. Garnish with chopped parsley. Serve at room temperature.

Refrigerate any leftovers; return to room temperature before serving.

Pacific Rim Chicken Salad

Miriam Morgan
Food Editor, *San Mateo Times*, San Mateo, CA

Earlier versions of this recipe were simply ways to use up leftover chicken. But this dish has proven so popular I now cook chicken especially for it. Grill, broil or microwave the chicken, brushing it with a mixture of soy sauce and Worcestershire sauce. Of course, leftover roast chicken is fine, too. You can vary the vegetables at will as long as they're crunchy: broccoli, cauliflower, carrots, celery and cucumber work well. The crown of crisp, puffed rice sticks looks impressive and is fun to eat.

Makes 8 servings

Dressing:

2 tablespoons chopped fresh parsley
2 cloves garlic, chopped
1/2 cup reduced-sodium soy sauce
1/4 cup sesame oil
1/4 cup vegetable oil
1/4 cup smooth peanut butter

2 tablespoons rice vinegar or white wine vinegar
2 tablespoons apple juice
1 tablespoon brown sugar
2 teaspoons ground cumin
1/2 teaspoon minced fresh ginger
Few drops hot chili oil (optional)

Salad:

4 chicken breast halves and 4 thighs (or 8 chicken breast halves), cooked
1 red bell pepper, diced or julienned
1 small jicama, peeled and julienned
1 can (8 ounces) sliced water chestnuts, drained
6 green onions, sliced or julienned (white and green parts)

48 snow peas, trimmed, stringed and blanched 30 seconds in a microwave oven or in boiling water
3/4 cup toasted cashews (optional)
3 tablespoons toasted sesame seeds (optional)
Vegetable oil for deep-fat frying
4 ounces rice sticks (available in Oriental foods section of most supermarkets)

In 1990 the impaired driving death toll was an estimated 22,084.

For dressing: In electric blender or work bowl of a food processor fitted with the steel blade, process parsley until minced. Add garlic; process until minced. Add soy sauce, sesame oil, vegetable oil, peanut butter, rice vinegar, apple juice, brown sugar, cumin, ginger and hot chili oil. Process until smooth.

For salad: Skin and bone the cooked chicken pieces. Cut chicken into 1/4-inch wide strips. Place chicken strips in non-metallic bowl; add dressing. Cover with plastic wrap. Let marinate, refrigerated, 1 hour or longer.

In another mixing bowl, combine bell pepper, jicama, water chestnuts, green onions, snow peas, cashews and sesame seeds; toss to mix. Arrange on a large, rimmed platter. Refrigerate.

In a wok or Dutch oven over high heat, heat 3 to 4 inches of vegetable oil (peanut, safflower, corn or canola) until very hot but not smoking. Add a handful of rice sticks. They should immediately puff up. Push around with a spatula until sticks puff up on all sides, just a few seconds. Remove to a large, paper towel-lined plate. Repeat with remaining rice sticks. (This step can be done ahead; let rice sticks stand at room temperature until ready to serve.) Let oil cool, then strain and refrigerate for another use.

Remove chicken mixture and vegetable platter from refrigerator 15 minutes before serving. Drain chicken, reserving dressing (marinade). Arrange chicken strips on top of vegetable platter; pour dressing over all. Toss gently to distribute dressing evenly. Top with rice sticks.

Panhandle Potato Salad

Beth Whitley Duke
Food Editor, *Amarillo Globe-News*, Amarillo, TX

This recipe could only come from the Texas Panhandle, the heart of cattle country. Sunday dinner in Texas generally features a pot roast. This recipe makes good use of leftover roast beef. I've started buying bigger roasts, just to have an excuse to make this salad.

Makes 6 servings

6 to 8 medium potatoes, cooked
2 cups cooked, sliced roast beef
1 cup sliced fresh mushrooms
1 large onion, sliced into rings
1/4 cup chopped fresh parsley
1/2 cup mayonnaise-type
    salad dressing

1/2 cup dairy sour cream
1/2 teaspoon garlic salt
1/4 teaspoon black pepper
Onion rings or parsley sprigs,
    for garnish (optional)

Cook potatoes as desired. (Bake in conventional or microwave oven, or boil.) Once cooked potatoes are cool enough to handle, peel and slice into generous chunks. In a large bowl, combine potatoes, beef, mushrooms, onions and parsley.

In another bowl, combine salad dressing, sour cream, garlic salt and pepper. Pour over potato mixture; mix gently. Cover and refrigerate to let flavors blend.

Before serving, garnish with onion rings or parsley sprigs, if desired.

Every week about 430 people are killed in alcohol-related crashes.

Roast Beef and Radish Salad with Walnut Dressing

Rita Barrett
Vice-President, International Cookbook Services, White Plains, NY

Super Bowl Sunday in our house invariably means a room full of hungry men. I like to serve cold food so guests can eat whenever they choose. Over the years I have learned that whatever food I serve, hot or cold, it had better be hearty. This salad fits the bill perfectly.

Makes 8 to 10 servings

2 pounds cooked roast beef, trimmed and cut into julienne strips
2 large bunches radishes
1 cup walnut or pecan halves
1/2 cup walnut oil (or vegetable oil)

1/4 cup orange juice
2 tablespoons cider vinegar
Salt, to taste
Freshly ground black pepper, to taste
Green onion fans, for garnish

Place roast beef in serving bowl. Set aside some radishes for garnish; trim and thinly slice remaining radishes. Add sliced radishes and nuts to roast beef; stir gently.

In a small bowl, combine oil, orange juice, vinegar, salt and pepper; beat until well blended. Pour dressing over beef mixture; toss to coat. Cover and refrigerate until ready to serve.

Just before serving, garnish salad with radish roses (cut from reserved radishes) and green onion fans.

Shrimp Pita Salad

Jim Hillibish
Food Editor, *The Repository*, Canton, OH

This salad stems from that canon of cookery: Hot summer afternoons are not the time to work over a steamy stove. Still, there are appetites to satisfy. Accomplishing this in a quick and elegant way is the role of Shrimp Pita Salad. The bread is filling, the shrimp delicate and cool, and the spicy dressing brings out the finest of both. Be sure to place the mixing bowl, salad plates and forks in the refrigerator at least an hour before serving. And don't forget the iced tea garnished with lemon wedges and sprigs of mint.

Makes 4 servings

2 cups cooked, chopped shrimp, well chilled
1/2 cup finely chopped celery (use inner ribs of stalk)
1 tablespoon freshly squeezed lemon juice
3/4 cup mayonnaise, well chilled
1/2 teaspoon curry powder

1 head leaf lettuce, rinsed, torn into bite-size pieces and chilled
4 green onions, chopped (green tops included)
4 pita bread rounds
Freshly ground black pepper

In a chilled bowl, combine shrimp and celery; sprinkle with lemon juice. Add mayonnaise and curry powder. Mix carefully with a fork so as not to crush shrimp.

Spread a bed of leaf lettuce on each of four chilled plates. Divide shrimp mixture equally among plates. Garnish with green onions.

Cut each pita round into eighths; arrange pita pieces around the edges of the salads. Serve immediately. Pass pepper mill at the table.

Note: This salad can be made ahead and refrigerated. Just don't refrigerate the pita, because it will become soggy. The shrimp mixture will keep a day in the refrigerator.

Every 23 minutes, another person dies in an alcohol-related crash.

Smoked Turkey and Pineapple Salad

Barbara Bloch
President, International Cookbook Services, White Plains, NY

I like this salad because it is so versatile. Although I prefer to make it with smoked turkey, it also can be prepared with plain cooked turkey breast or with smoked or plain chicken breast. You can substitute fresh pineapple for canned. If you use fresh pineapple, you can omit the pineapple juice from the dressing or substitute 2 tablespoons orange juice.

Makes 4 servings

2 large Belgian endives,
   rinsed and drained
1 can (16 ounces) pineapple slices
2 kiwifruit, peeled and sliced
1 pound smoked turkey breast,
   cut into julienne strips
1/2 cup mayonnaise

1/4 cup dairy sour cream
2 tablespoons Dijon-style mustard
Salt, to taste
Freshly ground black pepper,
   to taste
2 tablespoons snipped
   fresh chives

Line 4 salad plates with endive leaves, placing leaves in circle around outside edge of plate.

Drain pineapple, reserving 2 tablespoons juice. Cut pineapple slices in half. Arrange pineapple slices and kiwifruit slices over endive. Mound turkey on top of pineapple and kiwifruit.

In a small bowl, combine mayonnaise, sour cream, mustard, reserved 2 tablespoons pineapple juice, salt, pepper and chives; stir until well blended. Spoon some mayonnaise mixture over each serving. Serve immediately.

Spicy Corned Beef Salad

Marie D. Galyean
Lifestyle and Food Editor, *Idaho Press-Tribune*, Nampa, ID

The Irish traditions of my family always called for corned beef, cabbage and boiled potatoes for St. Patrick's Day and other special occasions. The next day, corned beef hash was always on the menu. For a change of pace, I developed this tasty salad, which is good with a crusty bread or sourdough rolls.

Makes 3 to 4 servings

3/4 to 1 pound cooked corned beef, cut into cubes

4 to 5 new red potatoes, boiled, cooled, peeled and cut into cubes

2 crisp dill pickles, coarsely chopped

2 to 3 green onions, finely chopped (with green tops)

1 hard-cooked egg, peeled and chopped

4 to 5 large pitted black olives, coarsely chopped

2 teaspoons spicy mustard

3 tablespoons olive oil

3 tablespoons rice vinegar

1/4 teaspoon garlic powder

1/4 teaspoon black pepper

Romaine lettuce and fresh spinach, rinsed, drained and torn into bite-size pieces

1/3 cup coarsely grated Swiss cheese

In a large bowl, combine beef, potatoes, pickles, green onions, egg and olives.

In another bowl, combine mustard, oil, vinegar, garlic powder and pepper. Pour over beef mixture; toss thoroughly. Cover and refrigerate 2 to 8 hours, to let flavors blend.

Serve beef mixture on Romaine lettuce and spinach leaves (or any favorite greens). Sprinkle cheese over the top just before serving.

Every 90 seconds, a person is injured in an alcohol-related crash.

Succotash Salad

Teri M. Grimes
Assistant Features Editor, *The Bradenton Herald*, Bradenton, FL

What's as American as the flag, motherhood and apple pie? Corn, on or off the cob! We grow luscious corn in Florida, especially the Silver Queen variety. A sweeter corn is difficult to find, in my opinion. This salad is a one-dish meal. It's particularly popular with men at picnics and potluck dinners. You could omit the pork for a lighter, vegetarian version.

Makes 6 to 8 servings

4 ears fresh corn, cooked and cut from the cob

1-1/2 cups fresh lima beans, shelled and cooked

1 large bunch (8 to 9 ounces) fresh spinach, rinsed, drained and torn into bite-size pieces

1 green or red bell pepper, coarsely chopped

1 medium-size red onion, finely chopped

1/2 pound lean raw pork, thinly sliced

1/4 teaspoon freshly ground black pepper

1-1/2 teaspoons ground cumin

1/2 teaspoon chili powder

1 cup freshly squeezed orange juice

1 clove garlic, finely minced

1 tablespoon fresh lime or lemon juice

2 tablespoons olive oil

In a large salad bowl, combine corn, lima beans, spinach, bell pepper and onion; toss until well combined. Set aside while cooking pork.

Cut pork slices into 1-inch strips; toss with pepper, cumin and chili powder. Spray a heavy skillet with non-stick vegetable spray; heat skillet. Add pork to hot skillet; stir-fry 3 minutes, or until pork strips are browned all over. Remove pork and reserve.

Add orange juice and garlic to skillet. Use a wooden spoon to loosen crispy bits while heating skillet over high heat. Boil until orange juice is reduced by half (to 1/2 cup); remove from heat. Add lime juice and oil; mix well.

Let dressing cool to room temperature, then pour over corn mixture; toss. Add pork; toss again. Serve salad at room temperature. Refrigerate leftovers.

Note: A diced, ripe tomato can be added to the salad along with the corn and other vegetables.

Thai Hot Beef Salad

Beverly Bundy
Food Editor, *Fort Worth Star-Telegram*, Fort Worth, TX

> *Beef is still king in Texas, but we're learning to incorporate international ingredients in its preparation. This simple salad from one of Fort Worth's Thai restaurants is a great main course for hot summer dining.*

Makes 4 servings

1-1/2 pounds beef round steak
1/4 cup fish sauce (see note)
6 tablespoons lemon juice
1 cup thinly sliced red onion

1 cup chopped green onions
   (including some green tops)
1 to 3 serrano chilies, diced
1 teaspoon granulated sugar
Iceberg lettuce, cut into 4 wedges

Grill the steak on the barbecue or in a skillet on top of the stove. Do not overcook — the meat should be medium-rare.

Slice beef as thin as possible.

In a large serving bowl, combine sliced beef, fish sauce, lemon juice, red onion, green onions, chilies and sugar. Toss well. (Use as many serrano chilies as you like. One chili gives a mild heat to the dish.)

Serve each portion of beef salad with a wedge of lettuce on the side. Each diner should roll the salad in lettuce leaves and eat it like a burrito.

Note: Fish sauce, called "nam pla" by the Thai and "nuoc mam" by the Vietnamese, is available at Oriental groceries and in the international section of some supermarkets.

Tulsa Taco Salad

Paula M. Galusha
Free-Lance Writer, Tulsa, OK

> *When we moved to Tulsa from the New York City area 10 years ago, I asked several new friends for their recipes for Taco Salad. No one had a recipe because, "You just make it." After several tries, I developed a recipe my family liked. It has since been used for church dinners, women's luncheons and meals for friends and family. With the availability of numerous "lite" products, I revised the recipe — and no one has noticed any difference!*

Nearly 250,000 people died in alcohol-related crashes in the 1980s.

Dressing:

3/4 cup vegetable oil

1/4 cup red wine vinegar

1 tablespoon tomato paste

1/2 teaspoon granulated sugar

1/4 teaspoon salt

1/4 teaspoon dried oregano

Black pepper, to taste

Salad:

1 pound ground raw turkey

3/4 cup chopped onion

2 cloves garlic, minced

1 can (15-1/2 ounces) red kidney
beans, drained

1/4 cup water

1/2 of a 1-1/4-ounce envelope
taco seasoning mix

1/4 teaspoon salt

1 head iceberg lettuce, coarsely
chopped

2 cups coarsely chopped leaf
lettuce

1 cup coarsely chopped red
cabbage

1/2 cup sliced green onions

1 cup chopped tomatoes

4 to 6 ounces low-fat Cheddar
cheese, grated

3/4 cup bottled taco sauce

1/2 cup light sour cream

2 cups coarsely crumbled corn or
nacho cheese chips

For dressing: In a jar with a tight-fitting lid, combine oil, vinegar, tomato paste, sugar, salt, oregano and pepper; mix well. Store in refrigerator.

For salad: In a large non-stick skillet, cook ground turkey, onion and garlic over medium heat until onion is transparent. Add beans, 1/4 cup of the dressing, water, taco seasoning mix and salt. Reduce heat; simmer 15 minutes. Let cool.

In a large salad bowl, layer iceberg lettuce, leaf lettuce, cabbage and green onions. Top with turkey mixture. Top with layers of tomatoes, cheese, taco sauce, sour cream and corn chips. Pour remaining dressing over all; toss gently. Serve immediately.

Tuna Jack

John J. Poister
Executive Editor, International News Features Network, New York, NY

Tuna, straight from the can, is the base for appetizers, snacks, sandwiches and salads. Along with hot dogs, apple pie, corn on the cob and pumpkins, tuna is about as American a food staple as you can get. Here is a tuna salad recipe that will satisfy a robust, hearty appetite, yet it has many subtle flavor overtones.

Makes 2 servings

2 cans (7 ounces each) solid white or light tuna, well drained

8 pimento-stuffed green olives, sliced

6 midget sweet gherkins, chopped

1 teaspoon capers

6 tablespoons mayonnaise

2 tablespoons chopped fresh dill

Freshly ground black pepper

Celery salt, to taste

2 hard-cooked eggs, peeled and sliced

Paprika

Bibb or Boston lettuce

Place tuna in a small mixing bowl and flake with a fork. Blend in olives, gherkins and capers. Add mayonnaise, dill, pepper and celery salt; mix well. Garnish with egg slices; sprinkle with paprika. Refrigerate, covered, 1 to 2 hours. Serve chilled tuna salad on beds of lettuce on chilled plates.

15 fewer people die in alcohol-related crashes every day since MADD began in 1980.

Turkey and Barley Deluxe

Lorrie Guttman
Food Editor, *Tallahassee Democrat*, Tallahassee, FL

This salad was the result of a fortuitous combination of ingredients that I happened to have on hand. I had been intending to incorporate barley into my menus because it is so nutritious, but I had never gotten around to using the box that was sitting on the shelf. One day, I read a recipe for a chicken and barley salad. That night, I created my own version — Turkey and Barley Deluxe. I used less yogurt than the original recipe, substituted pimento for red bell pepper, and corn for water chestnuts. The barley is a welcome change from rice or pasta; it's a bit chewy and has an almost nutty flavor.

Makes 6 servings

1 carton (8 ounces) plain low-fat yogurt (use less if you like your salad less saucy)

2 tablespoons reduced-sodium soy sauce

1 small clove garlic, finely minced

1/2 teaspoon ground ginger

3 cups cooked barley, cooled (I use the quick-cooking kind)

3/4 pound cooked turkey breast, cubed

1 package (10 ounces) frozen pea pods, cooked and well drained

1 cup cooked corn (best if taken from fresh ears of corn)

1 jar (2 ounces) diced pimentos, drained

Lettuce leaves

Freshly ground black pepper

In a large bowl, combine yogurt, soy sauce, garlic and ginger; mix well. Stir in barley, turkey, pea pods, corn and pimentos; mix until evenly coated. Refrigerate, covered, several hours or overnight. Serve on lettuce leaves. Season to taste with pepper.

Wild Rice and Tuna Salad

Patricia G. Gray
News Assistant, *The Express*, Easton, PA

My husband and I love wild rice, but it is expensive so I try to combine it with more economical ingredients. I have discovered that tuna and wild rice make a tasty yet economical combination. I serve this salad with homemade bread sticks, iced tea and fresh fruit for dessert. It's a great lunch or light supper.

Makes 2 servings

1 cup wild rice, cooked and cooled	1/4 cup dairy sour cream
1 can (6-3/4 ounces) water-pack tuna, drained and flaked	1/4 cup mayonnaise
	1 tablespoon lemon juice
2 ounces fresh mushrooms, sliced	1/2 teaspoon grated lemon peel
1/4 cup chopped celery	1/2 teaspoon curry powder
1/4 cup chopped red bell pepper	Pinch dried oregano
1 green onion, sliced	Pinch dried thyme

In a medium bowl, combine rice, tuna, mushrooms, celery, bell pepper and green onion. Mix well.

In a small bowl, combine sour cream, mayonnaise, lemon juice, lemon peel, curry powder, oregano and thyme. Mix well.

Pour sour cream mixture over rice mixture. Toss gently. Cover and refrigerate. Serve chilled.

Even one drunk driving death is too many.

SALAD
DRESSINGS

Bacon Dressing

June Ann Gladfelter
Managing Editor/Features, *The Express*, Easton, PA

The most difficult part of preparing this recipe is finding the fresh spinach on which to put the dressing. When the spinach is available, just clean and dry it and pour the hot dressing over it. This Pennsylvania Dutch dressing also is traditionally served over freshly picked dandelion greens in early spring. It also can be used on endive and other kinds of lettuce.

Makes 1-1/2 cups

5 slices bacon
1/2 cup granulated sugar
1/2 teaspoon salt
1 tablespoon cornstarch

1 egg, beaten
1/4 cup cider vinegar
1 cup water

Fry or broil bacon until crisp. Drain bacon on paper towels; crumble and reserve. Reserve bacon drippings.

In a large saucepan, combine sugar, salt and cornstarch. Add egg, vinegar and water. Mix well. Add reserved crumbled bacon and reserved bacon drippings. Cook, stirring constantly, over medium heat until mixture thickens.

Pour hot dressing over fresh spinach or other salad greens. Serve immediately.

Creamy Ginger Dressing

Narcisse S. Cadgène
Free-Lance Writer, New York, NY

This is the absolute best dressing for a fruit salad — even one made with canned or reconstituted fruits, such as the canned pineapple or dried apricots with which we sometimes have to make do in the winter. Sweet and tangy, the dressing gets its zip from the ginger and lemon, and its smoothness from the sour cream. If there's any left over, I use it as a condiment for meats such as duck, pork or lamb.

Makes about 1-1/4 cups

1 carton (8 ounces) dairy
   sour cream
2 tablespoons honey

1 to 2 tablespoons lemon juice
2 tablespoons finely chopped
   candied ginger

In a small mixing bowl, combine sour cream, honey, lemon juice and ginger. Let stand at least 15 minutes to let flavors blend. The dressing will thicken slightly if refrigerated overnight

Dijon-Parmesan Dressing

Mary Beth Jung
Free-Lance Writer, Grafton, WI

This recipe appears in my "One Burner Cookbook" because it makes an easy dressing for a tossed salad to accompany many different stove-top entrées. I like to prepare the dressing ahead of time in large quantities and serve it with whatever salad ingredients I have on hand. It also is good as a marinade for a montage of crisp vegetables.

Makes 1 cup

1/3 cup olive oil
2 tablespoons Dijon-style mustard
1 tablespoon tarragon vinegar
1 tablespoon fresh lemon juice
1/3 cup grated Parmesan cheese

1 clove garlic, minced
1/4 teaspoon salt
Freshly ground black pepper,
   to taste

In a small bowl, combine oil, mustard, vinegar, lemon juice, Parmesan cheese, garlic, salt and pepper. Whisk until well mixed. Use over mixed salad greens or mixed vegetable salads.

"Discovered" Valley Ranch Dressing Mix

Beth Whitley Duke
Food Editor, *Amarillo Globe-News*, Amarillo, TX

When Hidden Valley Ranch Dressing hit the market in the '80s, many readers asked for help in making a copycat version. This combination yields enough mix for about 8 cups of dressing. The dry mix will keep for months in an airtight container. Best of all, it is inexpensive to prepare.

Makes enough dry mix for 8 cups salad dressing

Dry Mix:
1-1/2 tablespoons salt
2 teaspoons monosodium
   glutamate (MSG)
2 teaspoons dried parsley flakes
1 teaspoon garlic powder
1 teaspoon black pepper
1/2 teaspoon onion powder

For Each 2 Cups of Dressing:
1 cup mayonnaise
1 cup buttermilk
3-1/4 teaspoons Dry Mix

For dry mix: In a container with a tight-fitting lid, combine salt, monosodium glutamate, parsley, garlic powder, pepper and onion powder. Mix well. Store in an airtight container.

To prepare 2 cups salad dressing: In a mixing bowl, combine 1 cup mayonnaise, 1 cup buttermilk and 3-1/4 teaspoons dry mix. Stir to combine well. Refrigerate, covered, for 24 hours to let flavors blend. Stir well just before serving.

Variations:

Blue cheese: Add 1/4 to 1/2 cup crumbled blue cheese to 2 cups basic dressing.

Creamy Italian: Add a dash of cayenne pepper and 1 teaspoon crushed, dried Italian seasoning to 2 cups basic dressing.

Herb: Add 1 tablespoon chopped chives and 1/2 teaspoon dried, crushed tarragon leaves to 2 cups basic dressing.

18,000 people died in crashes where at least one driver or pedestrian was intoxicated.

Frugal Pickle Dressing

Jim Hillibish
Food Editor, *The Repository*, Canton, OH

Here's a salad dressing born of frugality. Its creator, a restaurant owner in northeastern Ohio, hated to throw out all those jars of pickle liquid after the pickles were eaten. There just had to be a use for it. And, indeed, there was — long before recycling came into vogue. Call it Frugal Pickle Dressing. This is perfect on fresh spinach, garnished with wedges of hard-cooked egg and thin slices of cucumber. Just remember: Be frugal in its use. This is a robust dressing.

Makes about 1 quart

2 tablespoons Dijon-style mustard
2 cups olive oil or vegetable oil
1 cup white vinegar
1 cup pickle juice, sweet or sour
   (from a jar of either sweet
   or sour pickles)
4 whole cloves
1 teaspoon salt
3 tablespoons firmly packed
   brown sugar
1 clove garlic, crushed
1 teaspoon dried thyme, crumbled
1 teaspoon caraway seeds
1 teaspoon poppy seeds

In a small mixing bowl, combine mustard, oil, vinegar, pickle juice, cloves, salt, brown sugar, garlic, thyme, caraway seeds and poppy seeds. Using a wire whisk, beat until well mixed. Refrigerate at least 1 hour before serving. Store in a tightly covered container in the refrigerator up to one week.

Green Goddess Salad Dressing

John J. Poister
Executive Editor, International News Features Network, New York, NY

Nothing works better during the dog days of summer than an entrée salad made with seafood. I have found that a homemade Green Goddess Salad Dressing is the perfect complement to such a salad. It gives a refreshing taste that is not too filling.

Makes about 2 cups

1 clove garlic, minced
3 tablespoons chopped fresh
   chives
4 anchovy fillets, minced
   (or 1 tablespoon
   anchovy paste)
2 tablespoons chopped fresh
   tarragon
1 tablespoon lemon juice

2 tablespoons white wine vinegar
1/2 cup chopped fresh parsley
1/2 teaspoon minced
   capers (optional)
1/2 cup dairy sour cream
1 cup mayonnaise
White pepper, to taste
Salt, to taste

In container of electric blender, combine garlic, chives, anchovy fillets, tarragon, lemon juice, vinegar, parsley, capers, sour cream and mayonnaise. Cover and blend until smooth. Season to taste with white pepper and salt. Refrigerate, covered, to let flavors blend.

Over half of all alcohol-related traffic fatalities occur in single-vehicle crashes.

Honey Dressing for Fresh Fruit Salad

Clara Eschmann
Food Editor (Retired), *The Macon Telegraph and News,* Macon, GA

Because fresh fruits are readily available in our supermarkets all year, they have become extremely popular in salads throughout our area. Instead of using sour cream or mayonnaise for a topping, a young friend of mine, who likes to cook and share recipes, suggests this dressing. It is delicious on fresh fruits with enough tangy flavor to complement whatever combination you might choose. I have used it on many occasions, and it always brings compliments as well as requests for the recipe.

Makes about 1 cup

1/3 cup granulated sugar	1/2 cup vegetable oil
1/2 teaspoon dry mustard	1/4 cup honey
1/2 teaspoon paprika	3 tablespoons lemon juice
1/2 teaspoon celery seeds	2 tablespoons cider vinegar
Dash salt	

In a medium mixing bowl, combine sugar, dry mustard, paprika, celery seeds and salt. Mix well.

In another bowl, combine oil, honey, lemon juice and vinegar. Blend well.

Using a wire whisk, gradually stir oil mixture into sugar mixture. Mix well. Refrigerate, covered, until serving time.

To serve, spoon about 2 tablespoons dressing over each serving of your choice of fresh fruits. (If desired, serve fruit on lettuce leaves.) Serve immediately.

Honey-Mustard Dressing

Carole Currie
Lifestyle Editor, *Asheville Citizen*, Asheville, NC

This tart dressing is excellent for cooked pastas and vegetables, creating an instant salad out of almost anything. It's wonderful over tossed salads or slices of ripe home-grown tomatoes or drizzled over a submarine sandwich. In winter I add a tablespoon of a dry herb mix called "salad herbs," which I buy at my favorite specialty food store. In the summer, I add fresh herbs, especially when I am going to use the dressing quickly.

Makes about 1 cup

1 clove garlic, finely minced
1 tablespoon Dijon-style mustard
1 tablespoon honey
1/4 cup balsamic vinegar or red wine vinegar
Juice of 1/2 lemon
1/2 cup olive oil (preferably extra-virgin)
1 tablespoon dried salad herbs or fresh herbs of choice (optional)

In a jar with a tight-fitting lid, combine garlic, mustard, honey, vinegar, lemon juice and oil. Cover and shake well to combine. If desired, add herbs; mix well. Refrigerate until needed.

Italian Salad Dressing

Beth Winsten Orenstein
Staff Writer, *The Express*, Easton, PA

This dressing is known as "Uncle Ken's", but I'm not sure whether that's because he invented it or because it's his favorite. He doesn't use garlic powder when he makes it, but I like the taste of garlic, so I add it. This salad dressing is good on a tossed salad, but it's an even better marinade for all kinds of meats, especially steak for the barbecue.

Makes about 1-3/4 cups

1 cup vegetable oil
1/2 cup cider vinegar
2 tablespoons lemon juice
2 teaspoons granulated sugar
1 teaspoon salt
Dash black pepper
Dash garlic powder

In a small bowl, combine oil, vinegar, lemon juice, sugar, salt, pepper and garlic powder. Mix well. Use as a salad dressing or a marinade.

Almost 60% of all traffic fatalities are alcohol-related on July 4.

Old-Fashioned Boiled Dressing for Coleslaw

Frances Price
Columnist, *One and Only Cook*, Baltimore, MD

> *At Robert E. Lee's birthplace, Stratford Hall in the northern neck of Virginia, visitors can chow down on real Southern cooking from May to October in a rustic tearoom run by local cooks. To go with the crab cakes, fried chicken and country ham biscuits, the cooks serve coleslaw — made especially delicious with an old-fashioned boiled dressing. This isn't the Stratford Hall recipe, but it comes mighty close.*

Makes 1-1/2 cups; enough for about 3 pounds of cabbage

2 tablespoons granulated sugar	1/4 teaspoon black pepper
1 tablespoon all-purpose flour	1 cup milk or light cream
1 teaspoon dry mustard	1/3 cup cider vinegar
1/2 teaspoon salt	2 egg yolks, slightly beaten

In a small saucepan, combine sugar, flour, dry mustard, salt and pepper; mix well. Stir in milk. Cook over medium heat, stirring constantly, 3 minutes, or until mixture begins to bubble and thicken. Stir in vinegar. Return mixture to a simmer. Remove from heat.

Gradually beat a little of the hot dressing into the beaten egg yolks. Add egg yolk mixture to hot dressing in saucepan. Return to low heat. Cook, stirring constantly, about 1 minute, or until dressing will coat a metal spoon.

Pour dressing into a glass container; let cool to room temperature. Refrigerate, covered, 4 or more hours before using.

To serve, toss dressing with shredded or chopped cabbage. Allow 3/4 to 1 cup dressing for every 2 pounds of cabbage.

Poppy Seed Dressing

Ann Corell Wells
Food Editor, *The Grand Rapids Press*, Grand Rapids, MI

My mother has always said if you have a good salad dressing you could serve it over grass — and this is good example of a dressing that goes well with many salads. I have prepared it with cider vinegar, wine vinegar or cranberry juice — whatever acid ingredient you choose is good in this dressing. Poppy Seed Dressing has become a traditional part of our annual Christmas Eve buffet. I serve the dressing over a mixture of salad greens, mandarin oranges and sliced avocado. It also is good served over spinach salad or a fresh fruit salad.

Makes about 1-1/2 cups

1 cup vegetable oil	1/4 cup granulated sugar
1/2 cup red wine vinegar, cider vinegar or cranberry juice	1 tablespoon dry mustard
	1 tablespoon grated onion
1 teaspoon salt	1-1/2 tablespoons poppy seeds

In container of electric blender, combine oil, vinegar, salt, sugar, dry mustard and onion. Cover and blend on low speed until ingredients are combined. Add poppy seeds; whir just to mix. Store, covered, in the refrigerator up to one month. Bring to room temperature and shake well before serving.

Sweet Indian Dressing

Paula M. Galusha
Free-Lance Food Writer, Tulsa, OK

When the dog days of summer arrive in Oklahoma, there usually is an abundance of home-grown tomatoes. This dressing turns plain sliced tomatoes into a delicious salad. I like to prepare this dressing because it can be mixed quickly in a blender and will keep several days in the refrigerator. Serve dressing over slices of tomato on a bed of Bibb lettuce. If desired, add chopped fresh mushrooms and sliced canned hearts of palm.

Makes about 2 cups

1 cup vegetable oil	1 tablespoon curry powder
1/2 cup red wine vinegar	1 teaspoon dry mustard
1/3 cup prepared chutney	1/2 teaspoon Worcestershire
1-1/2 tablespoons water	sauce
1-1/2 tablespoons lemon juice	1/2 teaspoon salt
1 tablespoon granulated sugar	1/4 teaspoon hot pepper sauce

In container of electric blender, combine oil, vinegar, chutney, water, lemon juice, sugar, curry powder, dry mustard, Worcestershire sauce, salt and hot pepper sauce. Cover and process until blended. Store, covered, in the refrigerator.

Tangy Tokyo Dressing

Narcisse S. Cadgène
Free-Lance Writer, New York, NY

This dressing is popular in many Japanese restaurants. It's not only a great break from American- and European-style dressings, but it is also just about the only dressing that goes well with a Chinese take-out meal. Although it's designed for use on green salads, I often toss it with leftover and/or freshly cooked vegetables for an appetizer.

Makes about 1-1/2 cups

1/2 cup orange juice	2 tablespoons lemon juice
1/3 cup vegetable oil	1 tablespoon ketchup
(not olive oil)	1 tablespoon minced onion
1/4 cup soy sauce	About 1-inch piece of fresh
1/4 cup rice vinegar or	ginger, or to taste
cider vinegar	

In a jar with a tight-fitting lid, combine orange juice, oil, soy sauce, vinegar, lemon juice, ketchup and onion. Cover and shake to combine well. Grate ginger; add grated ginger to taste. Mix well. Let stand at least 30 minutes to develop flavor.

This dressing can be stored in the refrigerator for two to three weeks if made with pasteurized orange juice.

Tuna-Caper Dressing

Rita Barrett
Vice-President, International Cookbook Services, White Plains, NY

I discovered this dressing by accident. I was trying to learn how to use my new food processor and was making tuna salad. But, as with so many new owners of food processors, I over-processed the mixture and ended up with a purée instead of salad. I didn't want to waste what I had made, so I added more mayonnaise and milk and used it as a dressing. Since then, I have made it on purpose. It is especially good served over a salad that contains cold, cooked chicken or veal.

Makes about 1-1/2 cups

1 can (6-1/2 ounces) tuna,
    drained
1 cup mayonnaise
2 teaspoons lemon juice
1 tablespoon milk or half-and-half

Salt, to taste
Freshly ground black pepper,
    to taste
2 tablespoons drained capers

Place tuna, mayonnaise, lemon juice, milk, salt and pepper in container of food processor or blender; process until smooth. Spoon into a bowl. Stir in capers. Cover and refrigerate until well chilled.

Yogurt Dressing

Ann Corell Wells
Food Editor, *The Grand Rapids Press*, Grand Rapids, MI

In these health-conscious days, we are all looking for ways to reduce the amount of fat in our diets. Unfortunately, salad dressings often are high-fat culprits, and it is difficult to find tasty, low-fat salad dressings. This one is not only tasty and low in fat, but it also makes a small quantity — just enough to serve two or four, depending on the amount of dressing you like on a salad.

Makes about 1/2 cup

1/2 cup plain non-fat yogurt
1 tablespoon cider vinegar or
    white wine vinegar

1-1/2 teaspoons lemon juice
1/4 teaspoon curry powder
1 tablespoon honey

Tie a Red Ribbon to your car during the holiday season.

In a small bowl, whisk together yogurt, vinegar, lemon juice, curry powder and honey. Refrigerate, covered, until serving time. Serve over mixed greens; fresh spinach and mandarin oranges; or orange slices, avocado wedges, kiwi slices and red onion rings arranged on Boston, Bibb or leaf lettuce.

Zesty Low-Calorie Salad Dressing

Norma Schonwetter
Syndicated Columnist, *Micro Magic*, Oak Park, MI

I am always on the look-out for a low-calorie dressing I can prepare at home. I saw this one in a newspaper and changed the seasonings to suit my taste. Add 1/2 teaspoon dried herbs, such as dill weed, savory, thyme or oregano, to vary the dressing to your own taste. This dressing clings to salad ingredients, just like the more expensive bottled ones. It has a tangy garlicky flavor and keeps well in the refrigerator. Best of all, a 2-tablespoon serving contains only eight calories.

Makes about 1-1/3 cups

1 tablespoon cornstarch
1 teaspoon granulated sugar
1 teaspoon dry mustard
1 cup cold water
1/4 cup white vinegar
1/4 cup ketchup
1 teaspoon Worcestershire sauce

1/2 teaspoon paprika
Dash hot pepper sauce
1 clove garlic, crushed
   (or 1/8 teaspoon
   garlic powder)
1/2 teaspoon onion salt (optional)

In a small saucepan, combine cornstarch, sugar and dry mustard; mix well. Gradually stir in water. Cook over medium heat, stirring constantly, until thick and bubbly. Let cool 10 minutes. Stir in vinegar, ketchup, Worcestershire sauce, paprika, hot pepper sauce, garlic and onion salt. Pour into glass jar with a lid or other container with a tight-fitting lid. Cover and refrigerate until chilled, to let flavors blend. Mix well before pouring over salad.

INDEX